One-on-One
   Evangelism

One-on-One Evangelism

By
JAMES H. JAUNCEY

MOODY PRESS
CHICAGO

© 1978, by
THE MOODY BIBLE INSTITUTE
OF CHICAGO

All rights reserved.

Library of Congress Cataloging in Publication Data

Jauncey, James H
  One-on-one evangelism.
  1. Evangelistic work. 2. Witness bearing (Christianity).
I. Title.
BV3790.J36   248'.5   78-18727
ISBN 0-8024-6068-2

Second Printing, 1979

Printed in the United States of America

Contents

CHAPTER		PAGE
	What This Book Can and Cannot Do for You	7
1.	The Ways of a Witness	9
2.	Approach Them Through Their Needs	17
3.	Go for Depth	25
4.	Be Alert to the Social Complications	32
5.	Appeal to the Ego But Not to Self-Assertion	41
6.	Offer Something to Crusade For	51
7.	Meet the Need to Belong	61
8.	Seek for Substitute Identification	69
9.	Play Yourself Down	78
10.	Zero in on the Feeling of Guilt	86
11.	Use the Power of Suggestion, but Use It Responsibly	95
12.	Reverse That Negative Attitude	105
13.	Love the Person You Want to Win	115

What This Book Can and Cannot Do for You

This book can help you to become a more successful soul-winner by improving your approach to people. The author feels that this is where most people go wrong. In business terms, their marketing is bad.

This book shows you how to approach people so that they will be receptive toward accepting Christ. Whether you put them off or bring them to the place where they will want to make the great decision may depend on your sensitivity to the needs this book describes. *People can become receptive to the gospel without your unduly pressuring them.*

The author is not just theorizing. These insights are being widely used by successful salesmen and public relations people in the secular world. You can learn from them. "For the children of this world are in their generation wiser than the children of light" (Luke 16:8).

You do not have to be aggressive or have the gift of gab. The author has had long experience in successful personal evangelism; yet he is inclined to be a rather shy, nonaggressive person.

However, these suggestions cannot convert anybody. No methods can, for regeneration is the act of the Spirit of God alone. But you can help make people *want* to make the commitment to God which enables Him to save. That is a giant step forward.

The insights of this book put effective soul-winning within your reach.

1
The Ways of a Witness

The Christian environment of my teenage days emphasized witnessing and evangelism. The Baptist church, the Salvation Army, and Christian Endeavor, with which I was associated, were constantly promoting open-air meetings and door-to-door drives to win people for Christ.

I participated faithfully, but for me it was a painful ordeal. In those days I was a pretty disabled personality anyway, largely due to the agonies of the Great Depression. I was insecure, shy, timid, and plagued with crippling oversensitiveness.

Every time I approached a stranger on the streets or parks or knocked at a door, I died a thousand deaths, knowing full well the rebuffs, rejection, and even abuse that were coming. In those days most Australians seemed to be Marxist indoctrinated, hostile to religion and the church.

Looking back now, I do not know how I even had the courage. Those personality problems have largely been mastered, but I surely would not be able to do that sort of witnessing now.

I had misgivings about such aggressiveness, anyway. To go uninvited into a person's home or life seemed to be an invasion of privacy, an affront to personality. Our leaders tried to reassure me by saying that any methods were justified to try to win a lost soul, but I was still uneasy. Even now my hackles rise when a present-day salesman of religion comes to my door unasked.

It also seemed so artificial. Since I did not know the people I confronted, I had nothing to work on. It was a matter of imposing something on them from the outside which was not geared to their life experiences.

Those cold approaches were most unsuccessful. Occasionally I would get a flicker of interest, and there were a few decisions, but even those never seemed to be deeply rooted. Other people did somewhat better, but it was a colossal amount of effort for so little success. I felt there had to be a better way.

After a while I began to notice that my success in winning people was confined almost completely to my own everyday acquaintances: my workmates, those I played cricket with, the friends I got to know at night school. Curiously enough, at first I did not see those people as candidates of my own personal evangelism. I sort of felt that witnessing to them would be a presumption on friendship. I just tried to be a good chap. Most of us were suffering from almost unbelievable poverty; so we just tried to help each other.

Apparently they noticed that my spiritual experience was buoying me up and that I was having some remarkable answers to prayer. They began to ask questions. And their questions gave me the opportunity to witness. Under those circumstances I felt OK about witnessing. I was not misusing friendship; neither was I imposing on my friends. They had invited me to share, and I was ministering to their needs. For the first time I began to feel good about soul-winning. No doubt it also helped my ego to know that, at long last, I was having some success.

As time went by I began to ease off the aggressive, cold,

The Ways of a Witness

uninvited door-knocking and the buttonholing of strangers. But then I felt guilty. Was I reneging on a responsibility because I hated to do it?

I began to study the scriptural example, particularly the accounts of Christ's personal interviews. I especially noticed that there was never any intrusion on people. Usually they came to Christ or met Him in a natural way. The aggressive hard sell was absent. He never seemed to be selling a product to them in an artificial way. His evangelism always seemed to be a natural result of His interest in them as persons, and it was directly related to their needs.

That made me feel better. I felt I was on the right track.

As far as the rest of the New Testament was concerned, I was surprised to find so little mention of personal evangelism. Of course, I was aware of Acts 1:8, where Jesus said the apostles would be witnesses. However, it was pointed out to me that the verse did not say specifically that they were to witness, but rather, to *be witnesses* (of course, being a witness need not exclude active witnessing).

It seemed to be a matter of emphasis. Their *living experiences* of Christ were to be the basis of what they said. That was what I had been experiencing myself. I had not begun to make an impact until my own life began to tell. At the start there had been a lot of emotional froth without much solid substance. My witnessing reflected that weakness. It was preachy, moralizing, and overreligious. But after a while, fundamental changes began to be evident: positive coping with problems, victory over discouragement, conquest of personality irritations, increased concern for the feelings of others, more responsible workmanship, and added diligence in my studies.

My acquaintances found the changes impressive. I did not have to make any claims. People began to comment and ask questions. The witnessing momentum shifted: people approached me instead of my having to approach them.

I think that that is the reason there is so little exhortation about personal evangelism in the New Testament epistles. Such exhortation was not necessary. People were drawn by the magnetism of the transformed lives of those early Christians.

The outreach of those days was the preaching of the Word. It made people aware of the possibilities of God's power. The living experiences of the Christians reinforced the impact and drove the message home.

As word spread about the marvels of transformation, the crowds flocked in to question and inquire. In that atmosphere the individual Christians were kept busy witnessing to those *who came to them.*

Of course, there was no talk of psychological needs then. It would be a long time before psychologists would get around to systematizing human behavior. Nevertheless, the needs were there, and the Christians not only promised satisfaction but exemplified it.

It was one of my psychology professors who drew my attention to the appeal of that early Christian faith to psychological needs such as ego hunger, belonging, guilt, significance, and identification, to name just a few. I was intrigued because I had assumed that this kind of approach was a quite recent development.

During World War II, I used these techniques all the time. It was so effective that I was called upon to do a tremendous amount of troubleshooting, especially in industrial relations in key industries, notably trade-union disputes.

My procedure was always the same. Abandon any preconceived opinions. Let them talk and talk and talk until I could see what the basic personality needs were. Frequently the causes of irritation they complained about were quite superficial. The real problem was deeper.

Quite often we could do little to remove physical grievances. In those terrible days, we did not even have enough supplies for the fighting men at the front. But by making the workers feel good inside, they became willing to live with the inconvenience. Production jumped.

I do not think that I ever manipulated anybody. There was neither soft-soaping nor strong-arming. I simply showed the war effort in terms of the best that was in them. They began to view their jobs as a satisfying expression of living.

I do not mean to imply that it was formal psychology that made all the difference. There were people more successful than I who had never taken a course in psychology. When some of them studied psychology later, they admitted that the scientific knowledge added greatly to their insights into human behavior and also sharpened their techniques.

Naturally I quickly began to apply my professional know-how to winning people for Christ. Long before I qualified as a clinical psychologist, I felt that the approach to witnessing should be geared to individual personality needs. But now I knew more about the mechanisms of those needs—what was behind them, how they were expressed, and how they could be satisfied. The fact that I was using psychological principles successfully in my professional life gave me confidence.

It worked well, eliminating much of the hit-or-miss approach of my previous efforts. I found I could zero in on the points of greatest need and show the relevance of the Christian faith.

Of course, I did not win them all, by any means. I did not expect to. Human action is far from being determined by any push-button operation. The ultimate arbiter is the human will, which was made sovereign by God Himself.

But I did get steady results, and I continued to do so throughout the years.

In the 1960s I founded and ran a missionary seminary in Australia called Kenmore Christian College, which trains ministers and missionaries for the whole Pacific area. While there, I emphasized the low-key approach to evangelism. Reports from graduates indicate that it has worked for them, too. Their pastorates have been doing well in spite of the absence of high-pressure campaigns.

When I returned to America, I thought it would be a good idea to tackle a pioneering pastorate myself, to test the relevancy of my seminary teaching. Thus Coronado Christian Church in El Paso, Texas, was born in 1971. The initial membership was twenty-eight. Since it was an autonomous, nondenominational church, it had no outside resources or support.

We really put God to the test. We decided against financial appeals, every-member canvases, pledges, and campaigns. My contention was that if we met people's needs and they saw we were effective in our impact on others, they would happily stand behind us in every way.

They did. We have never wanted for a thing. It was tough for a couple of years, meeting here and there in rented rooms, but by 1973 we had a modest but adequate sanctuary and education plant.

There has been no emphasis on getting great numbers of members. We have had no crusades, no lay-witness campaigns. No commercial "growth" organizations were brought in to help. The members were not hounded into personal-evangelism efforts. They were urged to take it easy, let God work in their lives, and unobtrusively witness to others as natural opportunities occurred.

My own work has been totally among people. We decided

we did not need an office routine, paper shuffling, committees, promotion, and so forth. From the beginning, I spent my time trying to help people, counseling, and visiting in hospitals, other institutions, and homes.

More often than not, I do not mention religion at the start. I just try to help, and I seek to determine needs. Out of this atmosphere evangelism comes naturally, but I never press it. Sometimes it takes months before a decision is made.

The result has been a steady influx in membership. After six years we had nearly five hundred members. This is not great as far as church growth is concerned, but the beauty of it is that it has been so relaxed and unpressured.

It is not just me. Recently the church was without a minister for several months while I was abroad. Nothing stopped. The work went on as before, with members even doing the preaching. So it is a solid work.

Actually, constant growth is our main problem. If we do not find a solution, we shall arrive at the place where we no longer have personal touch with people, and then we shall become unaware of their individual needs.

I like our present setup: no imitation of the commercial rat race; business at a bare minimum; committees only transitory, and then only for specific, one-time needs; not too much religious activity; and every function geared to needs.

Yet I am extremely busy, but not with overhead, just with people. It is a relaxed, fulfilling church. We have time to live.

Our modest success indicates to me that what I have just described is what most people want. We need a Christian expression that is effective but not arduous, where religion is a buoyancy not a burden!

Most of us want to be part of the soul-winning venture, but we are not salesmen. We do not want to be. We hate to intrude upon people, but we do yearn to contribute.

I am convinced that all of us can be soul-winners or can aid the process. And soul-winning can be achieved in a relaxed, natural way, provided we can sense people's inner needs and can lovingly seek to satisfy them by our wonderful faith.

Let us see how it works.

2
Approach Them Through Their Needs

Jesus had no fixed formula for approaching people. He was seldom theological at the start. His compassion seemed to draw Him like a magnet to human need, and He addressed Himself to that.

Often the needs were material: blindness, sickness. More often they were spiritual: bereavement (Mary and Martha, John 11:20-44); social ostracism (Zacchaeus, Luke 19:1-10); yearning for eternal life (the rich young ruler, Mark 10:17-27); and unsatisfied religiousness (Nicodemus, John 3:1-21). Jesus applied Himself at the point of the need; then, as the person was ready for it, He went on to the necessity of personal committal.

Many attempts at soul-winning fail because this approach is reversed. The unsaved person is faced with, to him, bewildering terms such as *repentance, faith, regeneration, salvation,* but he does not see the relevance of those terms to his need.

Jesus has not been called "the greatest Psychologist who ever lived" for nothing. He knew that people act only when they see ahead a promise of the fulfillment of their needs. So He worked on meeting needs first.

He also knew that theological truth is spiritually discerned. That means that in order to recognize divine truth we first need the Spirit of God to be within us. Since the Spirit does not indwell us until conversion, we should, as much as possible, leave detailed theology until after the person has been born again. Only the basic facts of the gospel are needed before then.

When approaching a person before conversion, we are wiser to limit ourselves to whatever is required to gain a verdict for Christ. However, although our first approach should seldom be theological, we must keep in mind that our ultimate goal is doctrinal and very much so. There is no way we can psychoanalyze the person into the Kingdom. We are not after a degree of change but a total spiritual rebirth.

Sooner or later, he must be made to see that without Christ he is lost, that his eternal destiny is at stake. There must be no doubt in his mind that he cannot save himself, that the substitutionary sacrifice of Christ can be applied on his behalf, and that his salvation will come through his repentance and faith. He must be born again, a work of the Spirit alone.

The initial task of the soul-winner is to create a favorable atmosphere for the reception of this message. If the approach is in line with the hearer's deepest psychological needs, he will be motivated toward receiving the message. He still may balk when the moment of commitment comes. That is an area where his will alone is sovereign, but we shall have done all we can.

Let us look at some actual cases of conversion. They illustrate how important it is to approach people through their deepest personality needs.

In a lifetime of evangelism I have never ceased to be amazed at the miracles of transformation that conversion

Approach Them Through Their Needs 19

brings. Yet as I looked at Edgar, I could hardly believe what I was seeing. His head was slumped over his arms on the deck opposite me. He was literally sobbing out his commitment to Christ. Yet this was the arrogant, know-it-all agnostic who had scornfully resisted me for so long; the self-made, eminently successful attorney who needed neither God nor man.

Ronald was an entirely different type—insecure, shy, fearful, defeated, and unhappy. Yet, incredibly, one Sunday morning at church, he left his place, braved that large congregation, and came down to the front to accept Christ. After that he was a completely new man.

Marsha made her decision in a hospital bed. When I first met her, she was a beaten, bitter woman. Her husband had abandoned her, her son was in trouble with the police, and she had had to undergo a mastectomy. For the longest time there was no rift in those awful clouds of depression. Yet now her face was beaming with the promise of a brand-new, exciting life.

To people who witnessed those conversions, it looked as if lightning had struck out of a clear, blue sky. In a sense, it had. For I believe that no matter how unspectacular the experience, there can be no spiritual rebirth without the miracle of the intrusion of divine life. But not so evident were the months of behind-the-scenes, carefully studied cultivation that I had put in.

During those preceding weary weeks, I had drawn heavily on all I had learned about human needs from books and experience. There had been no gimmicks or tricks, no undue pressure. Progressively, I had slanted my approach to what I had come to see were the non-Christians' deepest needs. I have long realized that this in-depth preparation is always required for total commitment to Jesus.

I have always felt that the faith of the soul-winner who

wants lasting conversions is something like that of Elijah on Mount Carmel. He did all he could: built the altar, prepared the sacrifice, and then prayed for the fire to fall (1 Kings 18:30-38).

When I was a very young Christian, so eager to be a successful soul-winner, I figured that God was so powerful that it did not matter what I did. So my approach to people often was careless and ill-advised, my messages poorly prepared.

I did not win anybody.

Yet I went on, confidently advocating to others, "Leave it all to God." Then someone drew my attention to the miracle of the feeding of the five thousand. Jesus could have fed them all by the mere wave of a hand. Instead, He asked for and used all they had to offer: five loaves and two fishes (Matt. 14:15-21).

From that time I have always tried to do all that I am capable of, just as if everything depends on me, whether it is a personal contact or a gospel sermon. At the same time, I am full of expectancy that the lightning will strike.

I still do not win all my contacts, but, in time, most of them do come through for Christ.

Let me stress at the start that I am looking for much more than personal reform. The conversion I expect is the permeation of the soul by the Spirit of Christ so that an altogether new spiritual creation is born. I cannot generate that. It has to be the initiative of God alone.

My part is to persuade the person to make that commitment to Christ (repentance and faith) that will enable God to act.

This makes it a matter of salesmanship. But it is not the high-pressure, superficial variety that often goes under that name—the slick pitch that talks you into doing something that you quickly regret when the salesman has gone.

No. It is in-depth salesmanship. You study the person so sympathetically and carefully that you realize his deepest needs. Then you lead him until his own insight tells him that Christ can give him the fulfillment he is craving. When he is convinced of that, he is eager to make the commitment. In fact, I often have people finally seeking me out to make that decision. I never hurry them. I just wait until, for them, the time is ripe.

In spite of my conviction that I must give evangelism all I have, I am careful not to do too much. Jesus was happy to use the five loaves and two fishes, but He did not buy a bakery!

When I was just a beginner in evangelism, I became very envious of an evangelist who visited our church. He was a dynamic, fluent man, a real spellbinder, and a great promoter. His advertising made his crusade the talk of the town. We had training groups galore and night after night of door-to-door canvassing. The results, in terms of decisions, were spectacular.

But then he was gone and with him the glamour. Within a month, almost all his converts had drifted away. It had taken me months of unglamourous work to win a few. But they stuck. I realized I should not have felt inferior about my small efforts.

This low-pressure approach directed to people's needs appears to be almost effortless compared with high-pressure evangelism. But, if anything, it calls for even more self-giving. It is completely dependent on the kind of patient love that is willing to cultivate a person's friendship over many months to such a depth that we get to know his deepest needs and longings. That depth of insight into what motivates his life is necessary so that we can tap his whole personality for God.

In this approach, we do not have to psych people into making a decision. Almost inevitably they will arrive at commitment on their own if we approach them the right way. Nothing could be more relaxed and low key.

Of course, whenever and wherever there have been people who care, there has been attention to human needs. But in recent years, in all walks of life, desire to persuade people has reached gigantic proportions. So much in business, social, and political life depends on it. Since persuasion has to do with getting one to see his needs, the study of human needs has received tremendous emphasis and has been the basis of much research. The result has been the discovery of principles that have revolutionized personal relations in industry, commerce, advertising, education, and nearly all areas of human endeavor.

I feel fortunate that, as a clinical psychologist, I have had to keep abreast of most of these current developments. Many are highly relevant to the soul-winner's task. Yet they are so simple to understand and apply that they are within everyone's reach. Indeed, these psychological techniques are so simple that one can hardly call them "discoveries," as we would radium or the electron tube. Even a child may use them at times, certainly without knowing them as instruments of human persuasion.

Neither are they that new. The salesmen, teachers, politicians, and persuaders of ancient times automatically gravitated to their use.

Modern psychology has systematically studied the whole spectrum of human motivation, evaluating each personality need in terms of its effect on behavior and working out the most effective ways of motivating people. All this work has been scientifically tested either in the psychological laboratory or in actual experience. Since literally billions of

Approach Them Through Their Needs

dollars are dependent on these results, nothing has been left to chance.

Consequently, there has been a tremendous refinement of the rule-of-thumb methods used for centuries. The effect on our way of life has been nothing short of staggering. To many of us, the impact may be too great for our own good. Psychology is no respecter of persons. Bad men can, and do, use the techniques of persuasion.

We can use them for God.

Of course, you can get by without all this. There were great soul-winners long before this research was even heard of. There were successful farmers, too, centuries before our modern refinements in agricultural science. In primitive lands, they are still surviving without modern technology. Yet what farmer wants just to get by, if he can help it?

The sowers of the seed that perishes have enormously increased their production by the use of science. There is every reason why the sowers of the immortal Word should do the same.

Jesus did. His ministry exemplified techniques that did not become known for nearly two thousand years afterward. But His wisdom should hardly be surprising. He knew human nature because He created it. We are only now beginning to unearth some of those techniques.

Now that He has allowed us to become aware of these insights, I feel He is waiting eagerly for us to harness them in His service, just as we are doing in electronics and many other fields.

But a word of warning. No matter how we sharpen our soul-winning techniques, we are not going to win everybody. Human behavior is not that predictable. Besides, our respect for personality requires that we do not manipulate people. But just as persuasion in the material world has been made infinitely more effective, soul-winning can be, too.

Research in human engineering has boiled down the basic human drives into several distinct areas. We are going to look at each in turn to see how it applies to the soul-winning process. But first we need to explore just what it is that brings about a lasting conversion.

3
Go for Depth

The parable of the sower (Matt. 13:1-9, 18-23) is about soul-winning. Here Jesus warns that if we are to avoid superficial results, we have to go for depth. We are to make sure that the seed falls into good ground, penetrating deep into the personality. If the seed merely remains on the surface, it will quickly be burned up by the sun or picked up by the birds. The mere circumstances of life will nullify our efforts.

This warning has profoundly influenced my soul-winning efforts. But I also have been intrigued to find that modern psychology backs up what our Lord said.

It is easy to bring about superficial decisions and promises of intent in most people, especially when not too much is at stake. But more profound and lasting changes require deep-seated operation on the depths of the unconscious mind. Only when the full insight of this hidden area of the personality is behind a decision can we expect it to last.

It is far more difficult to bring such a decision about than it is merely to persuade a person to make a decision off the top of his head. But without it there is little hope of the sincere repentance and faith that are always the prerequisite for being born again.

So we have to go for depth.

Everything depends on the *movability* of the *total* personality. This does not mean that the soul-winner has to do the moving. That would be artificial and ineffective. Ultimately, it has to be done by the Spirit of God, when the person is willing. We can only work on that willingness.

It will help if we understand that we are up against the nature of the unconscious mind, which is simply the storehouse of all our past experiences. It is the sum total of all that has ever happened to us, not only externally but also internally; it is our emotional reaction to the circumstances of life.

Of course, the vast majority of these experiences are long since forgotten, at least to our conscious minds, hence the term *unconscious*. But deep down they are not forgotten. In fact, they are very much alive. Experiments with hypnosis show that we never really lose anything, not even the experiences of infancy. We may not be able to recall them, but they are there nevertheless.

The unconscious affects us in many ways, but one of the most important is that it acts as a brake on personality change. The larger the accumulated mass of the unconscious, the more resistance there is to change and the more reluctance there is to change back again once a change is made.

This effect is similar to inertia in the material world. For instance, take two doors: an aluminum screen door and a bank vault door. The aluminum has so little mass that you can move it with a flick of the little finger, and a slight puff of wind is sufficient to swing it back. But the mass of a vault door, perhaps twenty tons or more, is so great that it may require an electric motor to move it. Once moved, that door stays put unless some heavy force is applied.

The human personality acts the same way. If the mass of the unconscious is relatively small, decisions will be easy but they will not stick. If the mass is great, it will take far more effort to bring about a real decision, but it will be much more stable when it does occur. This is the problem the soul-winner is up against, so it may help to analyze just what determines this resistance.

Two factors decide the mass of the unconscious: (1) the sheer number of experiences, and (2) their intensity. This means that normally the braking and stabilizing effect of the unconscious will increase with age. Children are manifestly more readily influenced than adults. It is much easier to win young people than the aged for Christ. Also, youth tend to drift from their commitment much more readily than adults.

However, this is not always true, and the other factor, intensity, also comes in. The emotionally charged experiences of life add mass to the unconscious far out of proportion to their number. The teenager whose childhood has been spent in the misery of the slums can easily be far more stable and mature than the middle-aged playboy who has had life too easy. The following examples will illustrate.

When I became a Christian while in my teens, my life had been a kind of private hell. I had never known anything but poverty, fear, cruelty, drunkenness, and neglect as a member of a large family that ultimately included fifteen children. I went through all the horrors of the Great Depression, having already suffered more than most people do in a lifetime.

It is therefore not surprising that my conversion involved a long struggle and heavy resistance. But when I did surrender, it was a deep-seated, all-consuming experience. My faith became so absolutely necessary, and so much a part of me, that it would have been easier for me to give away my right arm than to abandon Christ.

Therefore, it was hard for me to understand the superficiality of most of my companions. One week they would be enthusiastic Christians; the next they would be gone.

Trevor is a good example. He had come on our church scene like a hurricane. He responded immediately, and within hours of his conversion he was promoting prayer meetings, open-air services, and all other kinds of activities. But a month later he had dropped out. I asked him why. He was casual, disinterested. "I've given all that away," he said. To Trevor, dropping Christ was no more significant than changing girl friends! There was no depth.

With some exceptions (such as in my own case), Trevor's experience is par for the course in youth evangelism. Young people tend to be easy to win and easy to lose. However, older people differ in stability, too.

The oldest person I ever won for Christ was over eighty. Having spent most of his life resisting the Holy Spirit, he now went through an agonizing struggle. He lived only a few years after his conversion, but his faith remained as strong and unshakable as the Rock of Gibraltar.

Victor made his decision about the same time. He must have been about fifty. In his case, there was no struggle, no evidence of much previous resistance. When faced with the claims of Christ, he was immediately receptive. "Sure," he said, "it's about time I did something about it. When do you want me to be baptized?"

It was as easy as that. Too easy. He soon drifted off. Occasionally he would turn up, but there was no real involvement. Victor, even in middle age, had had it so easy over the years that very little inertia of the unconscious had been built up. The significance of all this for the soul-winner is that he has to take the bad with the good. If they are easy to win, most likely they will be easy to lose; if they are hard to win, there will be a greater chance that they will stick.

However, it is not just the weight of the unconscious that constitutes the problem. The orientation of the unconscious is also important. If it were naturally set toward God, maybe it would stay put. But it is not. Instead, it is turned 180 degrees away from God, directed toward self. That means it has to be turned. The task of the evangelist is to bring about the swing toward the Lord, or at least to get it under way so that the power of God can do the rest.

Both the Bible and psychology agree that, left to itself, human nature is self-centered from birth. An infant will not hesitate to grab a piece of candy out of another child's mouth and pop it into his own, quite indifferent to the distress he causes. With the passing of the years we try to civilize him a bit, to make him somewhat more socially presentable, but this is seldom more than a veneer. The awful havoc that is devastating our world is terrible testimony to the universality of original sin.

So not only is the unconscious the storehouse of experiences, it is mostly chock-full of *self-centered* experiences.

The good news of the gospel is that the Spirit of God wants to work on this unholy mess to transform it toward the divine image. But God's respect for human free will is such that He will not burglarize the soul to bring this about. First, there has to be commitment to Him in repentance and faith. In psychological terms, what this amounts to is the reorientation of the unconscious away from the self and toward God.

Actually, the derivation of the Greek word for *repentance (metanoia)* means just that. If a person had been going south and then turned around and headed north, he would have gone through a *metanoia*. Spiritually, that is just what has to happen.

The common idea that repentance is being sorry for our sins is too shallow. Quite often that kind of repentance is merely regret that the consequences have caught up with us! The repentance of the Bible is far more revolutionary. It is turning toward God (Acts 26:20), a whole change of attitude.

Faith, in the New Testament sense, is just as radical. It is certainly far more than mere belief, which even the devils exercise (James 2:19). Instead, we are told to believe *in* (Gr., *into*) Christ, not just believe Christ. There is all the difference in the world. *Believing into* calls for committal of the life; the other is superficial mental assent, which costs nothing. Belief is what we do with our minds; faith is what we do with our lives.

All this amounts to a complete reversal of the personality. Since this commitment is a condition for salvation, it becomes the focal point for the soul-winner's attention.

At first it looks like a colossal task, as difficult to accomplish as to move that massive bank door referred to earlier. Sometimes it is, but often we find that the Spirit of God has already been working on the person. Even though He will not enter the heart as Savior before repentance and faith occur, He does not remain passive. He is continually exerting pressure on the heart, wooing the person into making that necessary step.

This action of the Holy Spirit is itself an experience, even though the person may not feel or think too much about it. Since it is an experience, it constitutes a positive influence on the unconscious mind, thus tending to counterbalance the selfish elements. So our contact person may be much closer to making the swing to Christ than we might suppose.

Sometimes the time is more ripe than the person himself is aware of. I once knew a manufacturer who seemed so indifferent that I figured it would take a long time to win him. Yet he made his decision quickly and unexpectedly. Later

Go for Depth

he commented, "I guess I was closer to the Kingdom of God than I realized."

We can never tell. It certainly is encouraging to know that God is always preparing our way before us when we seek to persuade a soul to accept Christ.

Probably the most effective way of assisting this divine work is to keep the person under the sound of the gospel. The Word of God is highly radioactive, penetrating to the deepest areas of the unconscious.

Of course, there are many other positive influences, such as the person's own conscience, contacts with Christians, the impact of his reading, the effects of early Sunday school training, the background of the beauty of God's universe, and even getting his fingers burned by his own willfulness.

Such elements are more significant than they appear. They do not just lie dormant in the unconscious: they continue to grow and interact. William James, an early psychologist of religion, has called this "unconscious incubation," an excellent description.

We soul-winners can now see the profoundness of our task in clear relief. Application of what has been said above may save us from contriving decisions that are too quick and superficial. It should make us see that our thrust has to be on the personality as a whole, not just on that rather troublesome human characteristic that causes us to make impulsive judgments and regret them later.

This more thoroughgoing approach calls for a study of the forces that motivate the unconscious so that we may lever them for God. But before we investigate those forces, we need to take a hard look at some complications that could upset all our efforts.

4

Be Alert to the Social Complications

Jesus tells a powerful story in Luke 14:15-24. We all know that the point of the parable is that one ought not to make excuses to God and that the rejected Messiah seeks other guests for the Kingdom. But might we not also turn our point of view a bit and see something else in the parable?

The man in the parable scheduled a great dinner, but he seemingly neglected to check whether the time was convenient for his guests. It was not. They all began making excuses, whether or not they were valid. One had just bought some land and said he had to go and check on it. Another had acquired five yoke of oxen and said that he needed to try them out. Still another had just got married and presumably felt that his new wife had first claim on his time. Finally, in desperation, the host garnered a crowd of poor people who did not have such complications.

The soul-winner who is not alert to the complications of personal relations may find himself with no "guests," either.

A few years ago, while conducting a series of evangelistic crusades in California, I made a practice of personally dealing with likely prospects in their homes. Gladys was one of those prospects. She had been referred by the pastor because she had shown considerable interest for months, yet had never made a decision.

Be Alert to the Social Complications

I found her to be a delightful person, in her sixties, so cordial to the message that it was obvious that the Spirit had been dealing with her for a long time. I challenged her to accept Christ then and there.

"Oh, I'd love to," she said, "but I don't think I ought. It's Tom, my husband. We've been very close. He'd be hurt, would feel isolated. What we do, we always do together. You see, Tom has a thing against religion."

My first reaction was to tell her she should put God first, regardless. But somehow I sensed it was not the right thing to say. It would merely build a conflict of loyalties in her.

Since any direct approach to the man would be almost certain to be rebuffed, I had to find some point of contact that would give me an in. So I asked her to tell me about him. It turned out he had been in Australia during World War II. Since my own background was Australian, she gave me the point of common interest I needed.

When I called him up and told him, he was most cordial and invited me over. We talked a lot about the old scenes, but the question of religion did not arise and I would not have dreamed of forcing it. However, when I rose to leave he said, "Jim, somehow you've made me feel real good tonight. You didn't jawbone me about religion, but I have enough sense to know what you and Gladys want. Come by again and we'll give that a whirl."

On the final Sunday morning of the crusade, Tom and Gladys came forward together. Actually, Tom had been under conviction for quite a while.

The vital psychological complication in that case was that Gladys was more than an individual bounded by her own skin. She had developed such strong ties with Tom that in a real, personal sense they were one flesh. So the relationship had to be treated as one social unit. Failure to sense that unity could have meant losing a convert or endangering a marriage.

The importance of the social tie is also illustrated by what I had to do to win Tom. First, I had to develop a social tie between myself and him by means of a common interest. That rapport made him emotionally open to my message. It even broke down the barrier set up years before by an unfortunate church experience. Yet there would have been little hope if I had not entered that particular social orbit.

The New Testament recognizes this social tie and seems to imply that families should be won as families. Indeed, it looks as if many of the early churches were basically family units: "the church [which is] in thy house" (Philem. 2). In the case of the conversion of the Philippian jailer, his whole family was baptized "straightway" (Acts 16:33).

Personally, I have been capitalizing on this social element for years. In fact, I suppose that most of those I win are couples. When a man or a woman shows interest, I offer to come and see him or her at home. Then, almost always, the other partner is present. When I talk to them together, I stress that I want them to come to Christ as a family, not only as individuals. In these circumstances there can hardly be any suggestion of either one going it alone and entering an experience that the other does not share. This way the family tie tends to help them to decide in favor of Christ.

A man in Phoenix who has been unusually successful as a soul-winner told me that he always takes into account social ties. He is an insurance salesman by profession.

"If I persuade a guy to accept Christ on his own," he said, "you can bet your life that it will get his wife's back up. It may also make him feel disloyal. No. I learned that the hard way. As soon as I sense a glimmer of interest in him, I invite him and his wife to have dinner with me and

Be Alert to the Social Complications

my wife. Then I work on them both, as a unit. I seldom lose out."

However, it is not only the family that presents the complication. A person needs others, too. He has ties with friends, school companions, work associates, club mates, and community contacts. Even if he is unfortunate enough not to have those associations, the complication still persists. He still will have a *need* for them, and that need will color everything he undertakes.

A family transferred to our church for this very reason. The church they had been members of had no active youth group, and their teenage boy wanted to be with his friends, several of whom attended our youth fellowship. The parents rightly perceived that they would find it enormously difficult to have him won for Christ outside of his social setup, in some new group that he would have to begin to relate to anew.

This social contact complication exists not only because we happen to be married or have friends and associates at the time. It would be there anyway. The presence of others is essential to our very being. That is the way we are made. Even our physical existence depends on others.

Psychologically, we need people for love, companionship, mental stimulus, personality outreach, and personal fulfillment. When we fail to find a satisfying life with others, we wither and die. Life becomes impossible.

Any evangelism, therefore, that treats a person as a detached individual and does not consider him in relation to others will be geared to a false situation. Such evangelism will find that it is hard to win him in the first place; and, if it does win him, such evangelism may not have relevance to his total life. The areas untouched by his conversion will be enemy pockets menacing his spiritual flanks.

Take the case of Edward: aged sixteen, close family relationship, nominal Roman Catholic. A Christian school friend took him to a youth rally where he made his decision. His conversion devastated his family. They were neither bigoted nor fanatical, just overwhelmed and bewildered by an experience they did not understand. Predictably, they reacted to expel the alien invasion. Edward could not stand the pressure and dropped out of the church.

Of course, confrontations of this nature are sometimes unavoidable. However, this one turned out to be quite unnecessary. A visit to the parents, to whom I explained what their son's conversion was all about and shared the value of the experience to a teenager's well-being, changed their whole attitude. The sad thing was that this had not been done in the first place. Here the soul-winners were shortsighted in thinking that they were dealing merely with a boy called Edward. It was a person-plus-situation complex: Edward in a Roman Catholic family. The parents never did join, but they now gave him every encouragement in his new Protestant setup.

Actually, in the Western world, our family, social, and cultural ties are relatively weak in comparison with elsewhere. In the Orient and in primitive cultures, the individual often has extremely tight bonds with his group. These bonds may act as a kind of cocoon, almost impermeable to the evangelist. When becoming a Christian involves breaking these cultural ties, the results can be disastrous, leaving the convert isolated and often discriminated against.

The missionaries of the early church who went to strange cultures had this problem in mind when they zeroed in on the kings and chiefs. They figured that if they could win over the tribe as a whole, they would then have a favorable setup for approaching the individuals.

Where there are large, widely extended cultures, such as

in Israel, Muslim countries, and prewar Japan, this kind of overall takeover is not feasible. Consequently, evangelism among these peoples has been very difficult.

The trend to individualism in all cultures has brought about a weakening of the traditional ties. For society, this has been a mixed blessing, because the freedom from restraint has unleashed a flood of crime and delinquency. But it has made evangelism somewhat easier. The person challenged with the claims of Christ does not have so many inflexible social barriers to prevent his individual action.

However, I do not mean that we can expect a time when the social complication will disappear and soul-winning will be purely a matter of an individual and his God. Man is incurably a social animal, constantly replacing old ties with new ones. The big difference is that the cement that held the old order together was external, determined by the culture. Our newer social relationships are internal, conditioned by our personal needs.

The strategy of evangelism has had to change correspondingly. Where once we could aim at capturing the cultural setup (for example, the tribe), now we have to reach people through their psychologically motivating drives.

Earlier it was remarked that the social complications were inevitable because even if a person did not have significant relationships, he would be hungering for them. In fact, his need could easily fill the whole horizon of his mind, making him uninterested in anything else. The gospel, therefore, would have little attraction to him unless it had some relevance to his need.

Hugo had come to America from Germany to study business administration. At twenty-five he was shy, introverted, and quite lost in the mainstream of college social life. It was his feeling of insignificance that was eating his heart out.

He had sought me out after a meeting. At first I was fooled by his questions about various biblical problems. He asked them with great intensity, and yet showed an obvious lack of interest in the answers. At his suggestion I explained to him the way of salvation, but he acted as if he knew it already.

It was only after I began to ask about him personally that I became aware of the extent of his misery. He did not really need my answers. He needed *me,* someone to relate to, someone to show an interest in him.

Before I moved on, I tipped off some college Christians about him and got him integrated into a church group. He wrote me later to say that he was now a Christian and active in evangelism himself. His need had been met, so he was emotionally capable of giving attention to the gospel.

Somewhat later in this book (chap. 7) we will be dealing with the drive to belong, a most powerful motivation toward Christ. Hugo's case had similar aspects, but it was not quite the same. His big need was to be able to relate to people in his new American setting.

Akin to Hugo are those whose relationships with another have been cut off by death, divorce, or separation by distance. Retirement can do the same thing, creating a sudden cutoff from significance and from the group to which the person was important.

One widow who later became a most devoted church member said that she fell into a limbo of nothingness when her husband died. He had been a prominent man, and she shared that importance. Now that he was gone, she found that she did not get many social invitations anymore. When she did, she felt as if she were the odd person out.

Her response to the Christian claim was "Maybe, but what's the use?" It was only after I began to reassure her of her importance as a person that she began to perk up.

Be Alert to the Social Complications 39

It was not hard to do, because she was a talented woman. My talk stimulated her to venture out again to meet people and relate to them. Then, and only then, did she begin to show interest in my spiritual message.

Sometimes the complication can be due to economics as well. When I was a young Christian, a painter whom we admired very much was in our church. He told us that he refused to become a Christian for quite a long while because it might have meant giving up his job. As a family man in those depression days, that would have been very serious. The point was that his firm sometimes required him to paint pubs (Australian bars), which he felt might be wrong. Ultimately he concluded that what he painted was not his responsibility. Thus, he took the teeth out of the problem. Once he was convinced that his family would not suffer, and only then, did he make his decision. Up to that time, nobody could understand why he was rejecting Christ. No one had been aware of the complications.

If we really want to win people for Christ, it follows that we are going to have to face the fact that single encounters will seldom be enough. The tentacles of a person's life extend far beyond that person himself. So we have to get to know a great deal about him.

I find that people do not at all resent this interest in their lives. In fact, they seem flattered by it. So I carefully question them about their families, parents and grandparents, jobs, backgrounds, community connections, and anything about them that relates to their ties with people.

The way in which people respond gives a good indication of what their ties are like—whether ties are close, distant, pleasant, irritated, problems, or whatever. People's responses make me quickly aware of exactly what personal difficulties they will have if they do decide for Christ. Then I can sympathetically help them to count the cost fully, something that Jesus warned was very necessary (Luke 14: 28-30).

This kind of appraisal pays added dividends, too. It throws light on people's ego needs, which compose the most powerful drive in the personality.

The next chapter investigates that drive.

5

Appeal to the Ego But Not to Self-Assertion

When Jesus challenged those who later became His disciples to follow Him, He appealed to their egos, in the nicer sense of that word. The lowly peasant fishermen were told they could be elevated to becoming fishers of *men* (Matt. 4:19). Nathanael was promised he would see *greater* things (John 1:50). Zacchaeus was informed that his house was singled out to be the dinner place of the famous Teacher (Luke 19:5). The woman of Samaria was intrigued that she could be the object of attention of this Jewish Rabbi (John 4:9).

One way or another, either by word or implication, Jesus had the knack of making His contacts feel important, and He gave a promise of greater achievements ahead.

The appeal was never to naked egotism. There was not, at any time, any trace of flattery or anything like that. The ego fulfillment He had to offer was of a much more satisfying order. He offered significance, a sense of worth.

General Evangeline Booth of the Salvation Army used to tell how she handled the toughs who broke up her open-air meetings on the streets of London. She was a captain at sixteen, so anxious to succeed, but defeated by those hooligans in every attempt she made.

One night when her meeting was a shambles, she had a flash of inspiration. She called the ringleader of her tormentors aside and, amid tears, put her hand on his shoulder.

"I need your help," she whispered. "I'm only a girl and I can't handle this. I need a leader like you to control things for me."

"You mean *me?*" asked the astonished youth, growing taller by the minute.

"Oh, yes. Would you mind?"

The boy turned to the gang, quickly snapped out a few colorful, well-chosen commands, and there was dead silence.

From that moment on the meetings were models of orderliness. Better still, that tough later became a Salvation Army officer himself.

Evangeline Booth had succeeded in harnessing the most universal and powerful of all the human drives: the ego.

By *ego* the psychologist means more than the mere self-assertion we have in mind when we say "he is an egotist," although self-assertion is the ego's negative expression. The ego is the drive of the whole personality for fulfillment and recognition. It is the pressure to realize the satisfaction of achievement.

This all-consuming passion of the mind largely determines whether we are happy or unhappy. Happiness has been defined as the pleasant, emotional glow that is generated by the fulfillment of achievement. It is the feeling we get when we win a race, gain a promotion, receive an honor, solve a puzzle, or create something with our own hands.

Unhappiness is the emotion of the frustration of failure to find fulfillment. It is the misery we experience when we fail a test, become rejected or abandoned, get passed by for a job, or are snubbed or belittled. It is the depression that settles over us when we are living lives that are less than we are capable of.

Of course, some of our happiness and unhappiness comes from incidental circumstances, such as when the car will not start or when we get indigestion. But whether we have a deep-seated sense of well-being depends on personality fulfillment and not the mere ups and down of life.

The ego drive is with us all our lives. The toddler glows when he builds a sand castle. The schoolchild rushes home to show his report card when it is good—and hides it when it is not. The teenager agonizes to achieve his place in the sun and may resort to the pseudosatisfaction of delinquency when he fails. The employee tears himself apart with frustration when he is thwarted by small-minded supervisors. The wife languishes when she feels that she is losing her husband's esteem. The retiree begins to disintegrate if he does not succeed in finding new challenges. The old man sinks into misery if he concludes he is useless and put out to pasture.

One way or another, human well-being is almost totally concerned with this one drive.

Even the most pressing physical instincts seem to be affected by it. We need food and drink but feel bad unless someone wants to dine with us. Our sex satisfaction is largely determined by the sense of achievement that comes from feeling that someone loves us that much. The human craving for the society of others boils down to the fact that we need the significance of belonging, not just the association of people.

At first sight, such a thing as an ego drive appears to be quite anti-Christian. It certainly does crave fulfillment for the self. Should it not be denied or destroyed so that the attention will be on God and others? No. It should not and, in fact, it cannot.

The ego drive itself cannot be wrong, because God placed it in human nature in the first place. However, it can be wrongly directed, but that is a different matter. Abundant living without ego fulfillment is psychologically impossible. Since God wants us to have the happiness of an abundant life (John 10:10), it follows that His plan for us calls for personality satisfaction.

What He is against is the shortsighted attempt to find ego fulfillment at the expense of others. He wants us to gain it at a higher level: in service for Him and others.

We see this distinction in the incident in which James and John selfishly sought to corner the chief positions in Christ's Kingdom, which, at that state, they thought would be political (Mark 10:35-45). Jesus told them that their attitude was pagan; true greatness was in service.

Properly understood, true ego fulfillment is the significance of the "blessed are the meek" passage (Matt. 5:5). The Greek word for "meek" does not mean *passive* or *spineless*. It means *tamed,* as when a horse is broken in. Instead of breaking the ego, God wants to break it in, that is, control and direct its power to useful purposes.

Certainly the ego cannot be eradicated, at least not without killing the person outright. The ego is as much a part of us as thought or memory. To try to repress the ego would be highly dangerous to mental health. The other alternative is to recognize its existence and orient it toward God rather than toward the self.

Fortunately, Christianity is tailor-made for the needs of the human ego drive. It enormously increases the potential for fulfillment.

On our own, our yearning for personal achievement is blocked by our own inner inadequacies as well as insurmountable barriers in our circumstances. When Christ comes into the heart, we become united with the greatest power in the universe. That power enables us to do the impossible. We can achieve beyond our dreams.

Appeal to the Ego But Not to Self-Assertion

Someone has said that the Bible is the story of people who were asked to accomplish the impossible and yet did it anyway. Well said!

It has already been stated that joy is the emotional result of ego fulfillment. From that definition we can see what the "joy of the Lord" is. It is not manna that drops from heaven. What happens is that our Christian faith offers us this personality satisfaction, and the emotion of happiness is the natural result when we respond.

We can also see why Christians can be unhappy. Christianity does not give fulfillment automatically; therefore it does not promise automatic joy either. It simply provides the potential for it. Whether joy is realized depends on what the Christian does about the matter of ego fulfillment.

This psychology of the ego is a tremendous boon for the soul-winner. It is like selling bread to the starved. Only the need is much more severe and the supply infinitely greater.

Why is it, then, that people do not flock to accept Christ? There are two reasons. One is that they are not really aware either of the nature of their need or of how the gospel can meet it. The other is that fulfillment takes initiative and work, and most of us are not too willing to exert ourselves too much about anything.

So our task as evangelists is twofold. First, we must spell out just how our faith can bring fulfillment. This work can seldom be done in general terms. We need to know fairly precisely what a person's ego aspirations are and then show him how faith can give the answer.

Second, we must inspire the person to do something about the matter placed before him. Inspiration cannot be achieved by preaching at our man. He has to be carried along by our own infectious enthusiasm.

As soul-winners, we are fortunate indeed that joyfulness

and exuberance are the by-products of ego fulfillment. Everybody wants to be happy, so the promise of happiness or its presence attracts attention immediately. It represents success in the adventure of living. Unhappy people feel instinctively that they are failing in life. The ego is deeply involved.

My own conversion was due to the appeal of happiness. As a young teenager I was bored, restless, unfulfilled, and therefore frustrated, rebellious, and mischievous. Church and preaching repelled me.

It was the youth group that hooked me. I could see they were happy, enthusiastic, and purposeful. Their main thrust was not entertainment, but involvement in significant activity. They felt that Christ had given them a mission to win others and expected them to use their initiative to find ways of doing it.

In those depression days, the youth group and its way of life were the nectar of the gods to a boy like me. I had to leave school. I could not get work. My father had a notorious drinking problem. I felt less than nothing, unwanted, insignificant, and unhappy.

Now I saw a way out. As a disciple of Jesus, I could be happy, significant, and involved. I took to it like a duck to water.

Incidentally, youth groups that are geared to entertainment, without outlets for significant ego-fulfilling activity, are missing the advantages of this great incentive. Nothing is wrong with programs for pleasure, but there has to be something that provides much more in order for young people to be really excited.

One feature of the great evangelistic crusades, from Dwight L. Moody's on, is the challenge to people to achieve significant goals with Christ. They have been constantly told that their own salvation could result in the transform-

Appeal to the Ego But Not to Self-Assertion 47

ing of their families, their work situations, and maybe their whole community.

Adolf Hitler used the same psychology for evil purposes. It was enormously successful. He offered people the promise of being a superrace conquering the world instead of what they were at the time: a defeated, impoverished people.

The evangelism of the early church held the same kind of appeal. Slaves, workers, and the poor, who were treated like dirt, suddenly discovered that they were so important that the Son of God died for them. But that was not all: He wanted them as leaders in the building of the Kingdom of God. In their circumstances, who would not respond to such an appeal?

Since the Christian faith offers such wonderful promise of making a person feel important and his life significant, it especially is manna to the ego-deflated people who have been struck heavy blows by the adverse circumstances of life. There should be no shame in being victims of tragedies beyond our control, but the ego always acts as if there were.

Jonathan was a successful, hard-driving businessman when he suffered his stroke in his early fifties. For a while he had difficulty even talking. He became a defeated, broken spirit and lost all the will to fight. "I am just a carcass," he said.

I told him of the power of God to work miracles, citing case after case of recoveries I myself had witnessed. But I cautioned him against expecting God to limit Himself to the body. He would not be willing to work on anything unless He were given control of everything, including all his negativeness.

It took time, but the idea caught hold. When he surrendered his bitterness to the Lord, self-pity and defeatism evaporated. Now he was positive, full of fight.

Jonathan recovered well, except for a pronounced limp. He became Sunday school superintendent in a little Methodist church and tripled the enrollment in two months. He is that kind of man. What he is most grateful for is that Christ gave him hope and significance when he had lost all of his own.

Eva was fifty-three when her husband abandoned her. She was almost penniless, had no training, and had never worked. For a while she was reduced to living on help from her grown-up sons, who could ill afford it. She tried employment agencies, but they shook their heads.

When I met her, she felt hopeless and depressed. I could see that, drowned as she was in her own misery, talk would not reach her. At the least, some self-esteem had to be restored first. I scouted around and got her a job as a receptionist. At first, she could not believe that someone would want her services.

What impressed Eva was that I had felt she was important enough to go to all that trouble for her. Behind me, she detected the hand of a loving God. It was not hard to win her then.

Jack, forty-five, had worked his way up to vice-president when he was let go. His firm had been bought out by a bigger concern, and he was redundant. It was a bewildering, ego-shattering disaster.

Jack sent out a score of applications, complete with attractive résumés. He did not get a single response.

At first he could not see himself in any job lower than one at the vice-presidential level. Pride! Yet when the teaching of Christ was pointed out to him—that service was the important thing, not what you do—he readily agreed. Apparently he was looking for a good reason to save face.

Appeal to the Ego But Not to Self-Assertion

He quickly got a job working in a store, and only a month later he became store manager. Now, I believe, he owns the place.

He became a committed Christian, largely because he had learned what is really significant in life. In this area of psychology, we can never tell in advance what is going to hit the spot. All we can do is study the person and his circumstances so carefully that his real ego needs become evident.

In most ego-fulfillment cases, we are dealing with an already sensitive ego, which makes the approach much more difficult. The person's insecurity may make him misinterpret our good intentions and think of us as another ego attack!

One man, a contractor and an alcoholic, who had himself come for help, exploded: "What right do you think you have to dictate what I must do?"

Apparently I had slipped into being too preachy or directive and thereby succeeded only in arousing his ego guard. His outburst was unreasonable in the circumstances; yet emotionally it was quite understandable.

That example reveals what is probably the biggest single cause of a soul-winner's effort being rejected. The person approached feels that we are superior or that we think we are. It is therefore of the greatest importance that we do not give the impression that we know more than he does or that we are better than he is.

I think the interviewers at Alcoholics Anonymous have a terrific approach: "I am an alcoholic," they say. Those words immediately put the interviewer in the same boat as the contact, effectively neutralizing ego resistance at the start.

What I try to do is to explain that I have had a similar or related problem. "Yes, I know, I went through the depression." "I failed in my exams more than once." "My own mother died suddenly." "My kids had their problems, too, in their teens." "There was a time when I doubted about God, too."

All that is necessary is for us to recognize the unmistakable truth: we *are* no better than he is. But for the grace of God, we could have been infinitely worse. The person we are seeking to win will sense our humility immediately, and his ego will be receptive.

All encounters between persons involve ego clash to some extent, but it need not be so great as to be a hindrance. A great deal depends on whether the soul-winner himself has allowed the Lord to give him adequate personal fulfillment. If we ourselves are unfulfilled, our ego hunger will drive us to win victories over our contact. That is, we shall argue. If we allow that to happen, we shall have already lost him.

The contact will undoubtedly offer objections, but they have to be met in a manner that will allow him to save face. "I'm glad you raised that point. It is well made and I recognize the force behind it. But since you have evidently been thinking along those lines, maybe you have thought of this answer, which has helped me."

We are not being insincere when we answer in that manner. There is always something positive in every point of view, if we are careful and loving enough to find it.

As we proceed in this book, we shall see that the basic ego drive has ramifications everywhere. They are what make it so valuable to the soul-winner. Some aspects of the psychology we have discussed in this chapter deserve individual attention. One of the most spectacular is what has been called "cause hunger." Let us take a look at it next.

6
Offer Something to Crusade For

The apostle Paul was always a crusader, but before he became a Christian he championed the wrong causes. To appeal to a man like Paul, a much greater crusade than his current one was necessary. The Lord faced him with just that. He was to be sent to the whole Gentile world, "To open their eyes, and to turn them from darkness to light, and from the power of Satan unto God, that they may receive forgiveness of sins, and inheritance among them which are sanctified by faith that is in me" (Acts 26:18). Is it any wonder that such a magnificent challenge captured the imagination of this intense young man?

In the little church in western Australia where I was brought up, the most fruitful field for evangelism was the missionary meeting. We were often inspired by the testimonies of missionaries returning from abroad and challenged by the terrible needs they portrayed. At the end there was the inevitable appeal for full-time service. The amazing thing was the number of non-Christians who volunteered.

Many of the non-Christian volunteers had proved quite immune to our frequent evangelistic missions as well as to the heavy pressure we had put on them privately. Now they suddenly became aware of something bigger than themselves: to rescue a people living in heathen darkness. To that they gladly responded.

The psychological drive that was triggered off was the human need to identify with significant causes. It is a variant of the ego drive, for we tend to feel that our own importance is directly proportional to the importance of the tasks we are involved in. When the Christian faith is shown as an exciting challenge to achieve some great goal, it has its greatest and noblest appeal.

It has always been that way. The early church had enormous evangelistic success. It is easy to see why. In so many ways the church catered to man's deepest psychological needs and most especially to people craving to find something worthwhile to live for. The challenge went far beyond the appeal to mere selfish interests. The new Christian felt that he had been entrusted with the staggering task of taking the newfound gospel into the whole world. Even the possibility of persecution, danger, and death acted as an incentive rather than a deterrent, for it emphasized the importance of it all.

In such a crusade, a person could find worth and significance.

The awakening of modern missions at the beginning of the last century had the same effect. Almost overnight there came the awareness that a great part of the world was savage, pagan, and lost. Young people who had never before had more than casual interest in the church now saw a clear-cut purpose and a mission. They flocked to the fold.

Even those who, because of age or infirmity, could never possibly go themselves were caught up in the crusade. They saw themselves as holders of the lifelines for those who did go. The church had taken on new meaning and importance.

Of course, the crusading spirit has not been confined to

Christianity. Human history sparkles with the heroic tales of the explorers, scientists, and reformers who changed the world with their crusades. Crusading is inherent in human nature itself.

In a memorable article, *Time* magazine once described our present society as "cause" hungry. The hunger is more acute in our time, for the big crusades of former times are over. There are now no longer obvious worlds to conquer. So we will even settle for the ridiculous as long as it offers some kind of goal. Thus we have had crusades to use four-letter words in public, to put trousers on animals, to have night pedestrians wear red lights on their backs, and what not.

Apparently the need is that bad. We will latch on to almost anything!

That is why almost any movement nowadays seems to get a large following quickly. The opportunity for Christianity to capitalize on this human need, therefore, could not be better.

Unfortunately, once potent Christian crusades, such as foreign missions, have lost a lot of their appeal. Not only has the gospel already gone to most areas of the world, but some of these once primitive countries are sending missionaries to us! In several mission fields now, the percentage of missionaries per population is greater than the proportion of ministers in some of the home countries. Also, a great number of nations do not want missionaries anymore. So, at best, only a small number of potential converts can find relevance in this kind of appeal. (However, for people who are so called, wonderful opportunities are still available.)

What challenge can the present-day soul-winner use—one that will be relevant to everybody? Fortunately, biblical Christianity, rightly understood, is *itself* such a crusade.

The whole divine mission is the attempt by God to rescue mankind from sin and its consequences. The life and death of Jesus was a commando attack in that great crusade. The operation is still going on as the Holy Spirit seeks to apply the salvation purchased on the cross.

All of us are called to be crusaders with God to redeem the lost and extend His beachhead on earth. Our crusade includes both evangelism and person-to-person ministration to make lives happier and better. Such a crusade can be an exciting prospect to people who feel crushed into insignificance by the pressure of the mundane details of everyday life.

Betty was such a one. She was a good wife and mother, but housework, especially, had become a drudgery. It appeared so useless: cleaning and tidying, only to have the house messed up and the work needing to be repeated the following day.

"I'm just an unpaid domestic servant," she said. "What difference could becoming a Christian possibly make?"

"In your attitude," I told her. "If you want to follow in the footsteps of Jesus, you will have to regard yourself as His representative in your home. Instead of seeing chores, you will need to look at your tasks as offerings to Him. It will mean going out of your way to plan to say and do things that will contribute to the welfare and happiness of every member of your family."

The idea caught fire. Betty not only accepted Christ, but her whole life took on new meaning. Her passive attitude was replaced by an initiative to cooperate with Christ in her home. The transformation was a marvelous witness.

On one occasion I was dealing with a manufacturer who had little idea of what was involved in becoming a Christian. "Would it mean that I would have to become a missionary or something?"

"Yes, but in your own factory."

"You mean, me preach to them?"

"No. You would have to act as Jesus would; you would have to become personally involved in their welfare. It would demand a new attitude toward your product. Your business, instead of being merely a means of making money, would become, in your mind, an outlet to distribute your product, one of God's gifts, to people who need it."

That man accepted the challenge. He said, "Somehow I couldn't see much point in Christianity before."

Dennis was a self-styled radical. He had been very active in the college riots of the 1960s. Now all that had died down, leaving him deflated and lost, a man without a cause.

"I used to feel like a pioneer, sacrificing to bring in a new order for humanity," he said. "But it added up to just nothing."

"You can still do it. You could join Christ in His crusade to change your part of the world by changing people first. Of course, you would have to start with yourself. But you could do more good in the long run this way than if you threw bombs until doomsday."

"That doesn't seem like much impact."

"I guess Christ's eleven peasant disciples felt that way at the start, yet they changed history. We have to commence somewhere. The question is, What about you and what about right now?"

He was silent for the longest time, and then his eyes seemed to light up.

"Yes, sir. I'd like to be in on it, maybe become a Christian revolutionary."

Within God's great redemption crusade, there are always lesser causes of a more specific nature: overseas missions, the ministry, social service, evangelistic missions, every-member canvases, and campus commando raids. Each of them has definite appeal, and sometimes they may appear to be much more exciting. But if we focus on the lesser causes alone, the results are likely to be superficial and temporary. The Christian crusade has to be directed to making the *whole of life* an adventure for God. That way there is nothing to end or peter out, and therefore, no anticlimax.

Psychologists have found that for a crusade to catch on, it must have three factors: significance, specificity, and urgency. We soul-winners would do well to gear our challenge with those factors in mind. Neglecting even one could cause our approach to be completely ineffective.

The question of significance is two-edged. Not only must it be shown that a crusade is important; it must also be clear that disastrous consequences will follow if it fails. Human nature being what it is, it is the crisis aspect that carries the greatest impact.

In view of my own background as a scientist, I have often had the privilege of trying to win scientists for Christ. Among scientists, I have always found ready agreement that we need something like Christianity to take up where science leaves off. However, that has been too general to provoke action. Only when I have pointed out that science itself will be used to destroy us unless we have some crusade to change human wickedness have I been able to get any response. That statement focuses on a crisis. The hydrogen bomb is a nagging anxiety on every scientist's mind.

I have always found that the crusade approach carries considerable weight with a parent. His love for his children makes him a crusader for the good of his family anyway. The gospel offers him tremendous help in his effort. Yet the thing that gets to him is what his family stands to lose if he does not become a Christian, especially with the ever present specters of drugs and crime.

With young people it is especially important to stress the significance of the Christian task, together with the dire consequences if it fails. Many of them feel that the church is largely irrelevant to the pressing needs of humanity; yet they are very much aware of the crisis facing the human race. They have to be made to see that Christ is the answer to the question of how they ought to accomplish their goals. It is not hard to convince them of the logic that, in the long run, the only way to change society is to change people from within. Since only Christ can do that, our gospel becomes immediately relevant.

Specificity in outlining a crusade is vital because action can seldom be stimulated without it. That statement is true in all areas of life. For instance, an appeal to fight poverty may be readily agreed to, but nothing happens until you get down to specifics: raising funds to provide food baskets, enlisting doctors to form clinics, organizing employment centers, and so forth.

So, also, if we are trying to win a man to Christ, it is not enough to say that Christ needs his help to save the world. We have to show him that the basic trouble with the world is human sin and that Christ can cure that cancer. He has to see how the crusade starts with him and that then he is to work with a team, the church, to bring the transformation to others.

I usually pile on specific illustrations of how I have known salvation to work: an unhappy marriage that caught the magic of self-effacing love, a family torn apart by strife that found harmony, a work situation boiling with unrest that was calmed by the efforts of one born-again employee, a jealousy-ridden community that regained its sense of proportion by the unselfishness of one Christian man.

This approach of tying down the crusade to specifics also carries a valuable spinoff. It tends to prevent the convert from fading into a do-nothing, nominal Christianity. He has been made to see faith not merely as a state of the soul, but as a plan for action.

Incidentally, while we are on the matter of specificity, it is worthwhile to stress that the principle applies to what we ourselves say in the soul-winning encounter as well as to the goals we describe. We should be clear in our own mind just exactly what we want the person to do. To use terms such as *repentance, born again,* or *accept Christ* is foolish unless we explain clearly what they mean and how they apply in his case.

So much for the factors of significance and specificity. Now for the third factor: urgency. It is the time element, the pressure for *immediate* action. We have to convince people that now is the time for the Christian crusade.

Bringing about a sense of urgency can be tricky. For instance, we can set up artificial deadlines that defeat their own purpose.

The abuse of second-coming teaching is an example of such self-defeat. When I was a youth, we were often pointed to the signs of the times, such as Mussolini (the anti-Christ); Israel (the fig tree renewed); and similar prophetic possibilities, as evidence that Christ would return that year. The date had to be revised constantly, until the whole thing became meaningless.

The imminence of Christ's return is a solid Christian truth, but so is the fact that nobody knows the day or the hour. The importance for the Christian crusade is that we should be ready to give account of our involvement in it, knowing that the day of reckoning could be anytime, either by the second coming or by death. Attempts at biblical fortune-telling will not help.

Personally, I have found it more effective to explain the sense of urgency of the Christian crusade by what is hap-

Offer Something to Crusade For

pening now than by what is going to happen in the future. It is true that the crusade could terminate next year should the Lord return; but if it is not effective right away, someone is going to be suffering now. There is unspeakable misery around us all the time. That is the urgent incentive to action.

A final word on this matter of crusades. It might be asked: Why not major on the truth that the Christian crusade will save people from hell in the next life?

Such an emphasis obviously has all the factors of significance, specificity, and urgency; yet it can lead to superficial results. The reason is that many people are anxious enough to save their souls for eternity as long as it does not interfere too much with their lives here and now. We do not want converts on those terms.

The biblical approach appears to be to use heaven and hell as background teachings to put life in its proper perspective in terms of eternity. The foreground where the main thrust is aimed is the here and now. A *person* rather than a *soul* is saved. His salvation has immediate ramifications *now;* it then has its greatest fulfillment after death.

(Perhaps, to be consistent, I should be using the term *person-winners* instead of *soul-winners,* but I think that that would be altogether too pedantic.)

Anyway, my own experience has been that it is best to focus the crusade on people in their present situations, but yet make clear the wonderful thought that what we achieve will be for the whole of eternity.

In this chapter we have been explaining how we can harness crusade hunger by turning it into a crusade for Christ. In so doing we are satisfying a demanding human need. But a crusade is attractive for another reason. It also appeals to the instinct to belong; for crusades are usually joint efforts, and the Christian crusade most especially is. The crusade changes a group of associated individuals into a cohesive unity, and both the change and the unity are deeply satisfying.

We need to explore this need to belong next.

7

Meet the Need to Belong

In the moving story of Ruth, what was it that caused this widowed Moabite girl to leave her country and its gods, go to Israel, and convert to the faith of Jehovah? We get a suggestion in her famous response, "For whither thou goest, I will go; and where thou lodgest, I will lodge: thy people shall be my people, and thy God my God" (Ruth 1:16).

In those days a widow was much of an outcast anywhere, but how much more so when she had been married to a foreigner! Going to Israel had its perils, but the close-knit brotherhood there offered her an entity to which she could belong. She could find a place where she could say "my people," "my God."

We all need that.

John Flynn of Australia, itinerant minister of the Outback during the first generation of this century, not only was a great evangelist, but was successful in influencing the whole nation in many other ways as well. He was the man largely responsible for the coming of radio (pedal wireless) and the flying-doctor service to the hardy souls living in that awful isolation.

Flynn was under no illusions. He realized he would have been just as successful if he had had two heads. Back in those days, the lonesomeness of people was so great, with many of them hundreds of miles from their nearest neighbor, separated by a trackless wilderness, that they would have welcomed the devil himself.

In the case of those pioneers, the need to belong, to have close association with others, was more than just a need; it was almost an agony.

It was that pressure that bound so many of them to the colorful, warm sympathetic missionary. His visits could not be very frequent, but the people welcomed him like royalty. They could feel that they belonged to him.

From that relationship, the transfer to a sense of belonging with God was not a big step. They belonged to John Flynn, and he belonged to God. Thus the human belongingness almost automatically gravitated them into the divine orbit. Once they came to belong to God, their need to belong reached its zenith of satisfaction; for Flynn could be with them only occasionally, but God was always with them.

The need to belong has sometimes been called the *social* instinct, but it goes far beyond the desire for the company of others. In fact, we can feel the lack even when in the midst of thousands. Many of us have suffered from it in large, but strange, cities. As we have jostled shoulder to shoulder with the crowds in the streets, we have had the sinking feeling that among those thousands, not one cared whether we lived or died.

It can happen even in churches. Years ago when I was minister of a large church, I met a couple who were strangers in town. They had been coming to the services for weeks, but they were shy, disoriented, and desperately lonely.

At first, I found them to be rather distant. They accused the church of being unfriendly. But it was not really unfriendly; it was just too big. This couple was really pro-

Meet the Need to Belong

jecting their frustration at not feeling as if they belonged.

I came to know them quite well, and they quickly warmed to me. When I suggested that they go to an adult Bible class, they readily agreed. They took to it like a duck to water. Within a month they were Christians, and a year later the man was president of the class.

Incidents like that make me wonder about big churches. Would it not be much better if they were kept to such a size that everybody could know everybody else? Is not the ideal that of a Christian family to which people can belong emotionally and not just formally?

Where large churches are inevitable, I guess the only answer is subgroups: Bible classes, societies, fellowships, and guilds. Where they are effective, they become like little churches on their own.

One prominent reason we lose so many of the converts of city-wide evangelistic crusades is because they are left as spiritual orphans when the mission ends. The problem is so real that the Billy Graham Evangelistic Association, for example, creates special machinery to handle the transition to a home church. Such assistance helps, but at best it is a foster-home process. It is so much better if people can be born spiritually in a home where they are going to stay.

However, without the big crusades some people would never be won at all; so let us not throw out the baby with the bath water. The problem can be eased if each church has its pastor and representatives on the spot at the crusade, ready to garner in the new convert as soon as he makes his decision. That way there would be little transplant shock, and the convert would feel that he belonged at the start.

In any case, crusade-convert loneliness is not an often occurring problem. Without detracting from the obvious value of the city-wide mission, I must say that only a tiny percentage of our converts come through this avenue. Most of our members come from church or personal cultivation. How does the instinct to belong apply at the personal level?

My experience has been that it is one of the first aspects to be attended to if the person is to be won in the first place. Also, unless the convert is at the same time integrated into a church unit, he will quickly be lost to the church.

We saw earlier how powerful the basic ego instinct is. The drive to belong is an offshoot of that ego instinct, although it also has characteristics of its own. To belong is a mark of importance, something that adds to self-worth. The child says, "That's my Dad." A man states, "I am a Rotarian." There is an element of pride in both cases.

The amount of prestige of belonging to a group depends on what other groups are around and also on public relations. In one hamlet of about a dozen people, an old man proudly remarked, "I belong to the Checkers Club." It was all there was! In another quite sizable city, the garden club was the most prestigious. Its publicity-minded president had a knack for getting it into the news.

As we shall see later, public relations is vital in getting a favorable atmosphere for evangelism. Right here it is sufficient to say that if we want people to be won for Christ in a church, we must not only develop a church of worthy significance, but we must also let it be known that we indeed have such a church.

In most cases, the transition from being an individual to belonging to a church is too big a jump. The soul-winner is the bridge. First, the person to be won comes to belong, in a good sense, to the soul-winner and then, through him, to belong to the church.

Agnes was a widow over seventy, far too fat, not very well physically, poor, and almost friendless. Suspicious of the whole world at first, she almost froze me with her hostile, unsmiling stare during my first visit. I persevered and she gradually thawed out. Actually, she was not at all hard to win, and she became a most devoted churchwoman. Once she discussed the process.

"You don't know how important you made me feel, coming to see me as you did. Long before I accepted Christ, I considered you my pastor anyhow. Then your church became my second home."

I would say that where I have failed in my attempts to win someone, the most common reason has been that I did not first of all go to enough trouble to get the person to achieve a sense of belonging to me personally.

Such personal cultivation is always a problem to the busy pastor. It takes a lot of time and thought. Other less important, but more pressing, details tend to take precedence. Yet there is no shortcut.

Of course, most of us enlist the help of others. When I have had a contact that I could not get to myself, I have made a point of selecting a person in the church who has a common interest with him. Usually the two people will have similar jobs, but the common interest may be determined by other areas where lives intersect. For instance, both people conld be members in similar service clubs, both could be golfers, both could have young babies, or maybe they just live close by.

What having a common interest does is to provide at the start a ready-made tie, which can act as a beachhead for a belonging relationship.

Sometimes there is no immediate point of contact, nothing obvious that would give a common association. In that case we have to exercise ingenuity to uncover mutual ground. In chapter 4, I mentioned a case in which I discovered our common ground to be a country we both had known. Such points of contact are nearly infinite.

A learned professor of geology met a cleaning woman on a train. They were a universe apart until he noticed an unusual stone in her ring; then they had a uniting interest. An old man won a teenager for Christ after going to the trouble of finding out that the boy's hobby was collecting pictures of antique cars, many of which the older man had driven.

However, Christian integrity has to be safeguarded in this kind of approach. Nothing could be worse than to use it as a mere gimmick. It should be the mark of a sincere interest in our contact as a person. We are forging a real friendship, which we will not want to drop as soon as the contact makes his decision.

Once we have succeeded in developing this friendship, we shall have taken a giant step forward toward winning the contact. In fact, the friendship bond may well be all that is required. The contact may decide for Christ at that stage.

If his conversion is delayed, it is all the more essential to continue to integrate him into the ultimate Christian unity: the local church. We need to go to the trouble of taking him to the services and auxiliaries, introducing him around, and nurturing him in the church environment until he feels that he belongs. Most decisions are made *after* integration into church fellowship. Also, once the bond has been established, there is an added dividend, for then the convert will not be so likely to drift away.

Over the years, I have found it useful to put this belonging instinct to work by creating special common-interest units in the church. Young married couples' classes, called "Green Pairs," have been particularly successful. But I soon found that just a Bible class was not enough for them. They preferred a kind of society, complete with officers and social gatherings as well. What those additions did was to develop greater cohesiveness, which always makes belonging more significant.

A class or any other meeting, as such, is too loose to have much social appeal. Of course, it can be too tight, too, and then it becomes burdensome. Apparently people get satisfaction out of a group whose emotional bonds are sufficient to provoke loyalty and yet are not an intrusion upon personal freedom. We soul-winners must exercise enough ingenuity to provide classes or meetings that will just fit.

It is important that we keep alert to changing social patterns in setting up these groups. For example, in recent years I have been backing away from promoting groups segregated by sex. Fifty years ago, men's and women's separate fellowships were popular in the church. Now it seems that couples prefer to be involved in activities together; so that is what I arrange.

By far the most effective church social unit, in my experience, is the youth group. Here again, classes, as such, do not catch on. We first have to generate a sense of unity. Thus the young people can get to know each other so intimately that bonds are formed. Camps and retreats are powerful means of establishing unity and bonds, for in those situations the young people are isolated from their other ties and their social needs become focused on each other. Again and again I have seen teens go away reluctantly to a camp, largely indifferent to the group, and return as devoted adherents.

Since Christ is, or should be, the center of the church youth group, the drive that binds young people to the group automatically attracts them to Christ. Thus the need to belong makes young people in such a youth group easy to win.

It was emphasized in the last chapter that people are hungrily seeking for a sense of mission in life. If, therefore, we can produce groups that satisfy the need to belong and that have Christ's great crusade as a reason for their existence, we shall have a combination that is hard to beat.

As we have studied the psychology of human nature in this book, it has been obvious what tremendous forces we have on our side as soul-winners. So far we have given attention to the great basic drives, but there are other powerful motivating forces that can be harnessed to the gospel message. One of them is identification, which is discussed next.

8

Seek for Substitute Identification

When King David backslid so shockingly by stealing Uriah's wife, the prophet Nathan had a difficult and perilous task in bringing the tyrant to see the enormity of his offense. He succeeded in a most skillful way. He told David of a rich man with great flocks who had taken and killed a poor man's pet ewe lamb, an animal so beloved that it shared his meals and slept alongside him. The king exploded with anger. He would surely put to death such a compassionless man.

Nathan said simply, "Thou art the man" (2 Sam. 12:7).

It hit home, and David admitted his terrible sin. He had identified with that poor man and the way he felt.

The other night I watched a program on television quite some time after I had decided to go to bed. I was tired, yet I continued to be glued to the tube. The reason was that I became anxious about what would happen to a character who was having a particularly bad time.

What had occurred was that I had become emotionally identified with him—what happened to him was happening to me. I felt his anxiety, his fear, and his relief just as if I myself had been the victim.

Emotional identification is a curious characteristic of human nature. In our minds we may know perfectly well that what is happening in the story is certainly not happening to us, yet we feel as if it were.

But there is more to identification than feeling, because the experience influences action.

A woman who had come for counseling because of depression brought on by her husband's neglect suddenly announced that he had changed. He had watched a program in which a woman went through agonies of suffering because of her husband's indifference. The husband of real life said to his wife, "Darling, I feel sick when I think how callous I've been to you. I just didn't realize. I know how it feels now. I went through the sufferings of hell with that poor woman."

Psychological identification was a technique greatly used by Jesus. His parables paralleled events that could happen to anybody. The farmer could see his own seed being eaten by the birds, tares in his own wheat, and his own need to build bigger barns. The housewife visualized herself losing that coin. The ecclesiastical lawyer imagined his own prejudice driving him to abandon the victim on the road to Jericho. The truth that the Lord wanted to get across was branded on the soul because the people experienced the truth through flashes of substitution-identification.

Much of television advertising depends upon identification psychology. The appeal is greatly increased by the visual representation. We actually see ourselves in the exotic islands of the travel commercials. The clothes the celebrity is wearing seem to promise us his prestige if we only wear them too.

For us as soul-winners, unless we can succeed in getting the person we want to win to identify with being a Christian and at the same time enjoy it, the chances are that we are not going to persuade him at all.

It is not enough for him to know the facts of Christianity

Seek for Substitute Identification

intellectually. He has to visualize himself as a Christian and like what he sees and feels. In a sense he has to make a trial run of his emotions.

Incidentally, emotional identification is especially important in preaching or teaching. When we say that a sermon is dry, we mean that it is dry of feeling. There is nothing in it that we can identify with, nothing that generates emotion in us. Purely informational material is dry unless the speaker ties it down to our needs by specific examples or anecdotes.

However, most soul-winners do not have the opportunity to preach. For them it is usually a one-to-one relationship, which makes it all the more important to get the other person interested. In a one-to-one situation, the contact can walk away and the opportunity is lost; whereas the preacher has a more-or-less captive audience.

A great deal depends on how the person is approached in the first place, especially if he is a stranger. If we say, "I want to explain to you the plan of salvation," "I would like to talk to you about Christ," or "I have a message about your eternal welfare," most likely we shall be rebuffed. The words, on their own, would come over as too cold, too intellectual.

Suppose that we are on a plane and that we are sitting next to someone who seems inclined to talk. The best thing to do is just to listen at first. His conversation will soon gravitate to what concerns him the most. Then we have a clue as to what slant to take.

Perhaps he is worried about the effect that his business tensions are having on his health. He may say, "There are so many heart attacks nowadays that I wonder if I am going to be the next."

If this happened to me, I would say, "I know how you feel. I am a psychologist myself, and I see what stress can do. It has convinced me that an old-fashioned, vital religious experience is the only real answer to anxiety. Listen to this case."

Then I would go on to relate a heart-attack case in which the man had learned to live with his stress problems through Christ. You can almost predict the response word for word.

"I sure would like to find peace of mind like that."

In those few minutes, our contact will have gone through substitute feeling-experiences of a heart attack and of escape from it. Those experiences will create in him a powerful incentive to take action to prevent the heart attack in the first place by means of the Christian remedy.

Being a psychologist, such a situation gives me an edge, I admit. But being a psychologist is by no means essential. You could say, "Yes, I know how you feel. There was a time when I couldn't cope with stress either, but let me tell you how I found the answer."

If stress in this context has not been your particular problem, you could say, "Yes, I know how you feel. I know a man who was driven to the verge of a heart attack too, but it didn't happen and this is why."

The key word to the use of the identification drive is *witness*. When we relate the story of our own unhappiness and how Christ has changed it, we are giving the contact a living experience he can identify with. We can facilitate his identification by deliberately getting into his shoes.

One Christian lady, who had gone through a heartrending divorce through no fault of her own, felt that she had a mission to similar sufferers. She said that at first she was ineffective because she was still too sensitive to admit that she herself was a divorcée. All she could do then was to tell what Christ could do.

But the Lord dealt with her about her pride, and she

changed her approach. She would say, "I am so sorry you are going through tragedy. I don't want to intrude, but I was divorced too. So I thought it might help if I told you how I managed to survive."

Then there were immediate identification and quick impact.

Our experience does not have to be the same as our contact's, although it helps if it is. We could say, "I know what heartache means. My boy got into the wrong crowd and I thought I would go out of my mind. The Lord gave me a great deliverance when I turned to Him; so I figured my experience might help you in your trouble."

Perhaps we could put it: "I know how you feel. Divorce is a kind of bereavement. You see, my husband died."

Even if we have had no tragedy of similar agony, we can explain, "I'm so sorry. I've had times when I've been at the end of my tether too, such as when—" Then we can go on to witness about some incident in which the Lord delivered us.

Relating our experience to our contact's is another area where specificity as discussed previously is so important. People do not identify with generalities, only with specific cases. There is a vast difference in this respect between saying, "Christ saves alcoholics" and "John Jones was an alcoholic who lost his health, his job, and his family, and the Lord delivered him."

Thus the identification technique consists of relating a real-life experience that ended in the desired goal of becoming a Christian, and then getting the contact to relive that experience emotionally, with the hope that he will follow through to the same decision. But whether a decision for Christ will, in fact, occur depends in part on the emotional charge present.

However, what I have just said does not mean that the

greater the emotion, the greater the impact. There is a point where emotion becomes melodrama and causes people to walk away—figuratively if not literally.

I knew an evangelist who regularly broke into tears during his illustrations. It was far too much to identify with, and, in fact, we were quite embarrassed by it.

Another man had quite a good approach until he started to use an illustration or to witness. Then he would go into theatrics, hamming it up so much that we just wanted to laugh. We could not possibly identify.

The solution is to relive the anecdote experience first, before we ever use it. If it evokes sincere but measured feeling on our part, it probably will do the same for others. There are some experiences I never relate, even though they could be very relevant indeed. I was hurt so much when they originally happened that I still overact at the thought of them. There are others that appear to be appropriate on the face of it, but over the years they have lost the power to move me. They will not do either.

At the time when I was being confronted with the claims of Christ, I used to go to testimony meetings. I can remember three testimonies that relate to this matter of anecdotes.

One man gave a dramatic account of how he had barely escaped death in a train wreck. He had intended to catch that very train but had missed it. He cited his missing the train as evidence of God's intervening care, and he added that if we would accept Him we could count on the same providence.

It occurred to me immediately that since others on that train were not saved from death, it was impertinence to imagine that God will always intervene. But apart from the moral of his story, there was a smugness about the man that implied that he was a special favorite of God's. I could not identify.

Therefore, the point of the incident we use as a witness must be realistic. Also, it must be told in such a way that we do not appear to be boasting.

The second testimony that occurs to me was that of a man who told of his struggle to give up going to football games. He said that it was only after he had made this sacrifice that he was able to accept Christ and find peace.

The trouble with that story was that the whole thing was too trivial for me to identify with. I could not see why watching football was a problem, or that giving it up was a big deal.

Now, of course, I realize it could have been of vital importance to the man concerned. These things are relative. Everyone has to follow his own conscience. But it was not the kind of story to use in witness, because others could not be expected to feel the same way.

We all have our pet taboos, but unless they are generally recognized as taboos and we have sound biblical justification for calling them taboos, it is better to keep them to ourselves. As soul-winners the emphasis is not on Christian victories as such, but rather on those victories with which people can be expected to identify. The key is significance.

The third man, a Welshman, told with head bowed and in simple, unaffected language of the drudgery of working in the coal mines and of how after accepting Christ he had found a way to a better life. His new faith had given him courage to go on, knowing now that with God on his side, he could succeed. I sensed his deep sincerity, and since I, too, knew hopelessness (the misery of the Great Depression), I quickly identified and the message got through.

His story had humility, significance, and relevance, a

combination that seldom fails to draw us into emotional identification.

Perhaps the most effective way to use the psychology of identification is to get the person to identify with Christ Himself. My early Sunday school teachers were skillful at that. Through the vividness of their portrayal, I wandered through the Holy Land in Christ's sandals, felt the sting of His persecutors, the sorrow of His tragic aloneness, and the pain of His terrible death. Those images are still as vivid today, over forty years later, as they were when I was a child. When the going gets tough, I still relive them as an incentive to Christian living.

I have often used identification with Christ as a means of breaking down hostility. One university student was bitter because a Christian had lied about him and cost him his job. "If that's what Christianity is like, I want nothing of it," he said savagely.

"It's too bad that a thing like that could happen," I said. "But at least it will help you to understand how Jesus felt when He was treated the same way."

I told him of the last days of Jesus' life, and how malice, lies, and selfish vested interest had sent Him to the cross. As that student identified, his anger defused and he was ready to listen sympathetically.

Incidentally, that incident illustrates an important principle in soul-winning. Never get on the defensive. Absorb the criticism. Point to Christ and the hostility will dissolve.

Especially with young people, the unselfish, crusading zeal of Jesus has particular appeal. As we have seen when dealing with cause hunger (chap. 4), crusading is right down their alley. It enables them to identify readily.

When I was a university student, we had a former Communist in our Christian fellowship. His conversion occurred pretty much on his own. He had read the gospel of

Seek for Substitute Identification

Mark and simply became emotionally identified with Christ in that gripping account.

The identification approach to soul-winning means having compassion on people just as the Lord did. We have to get into their skins until we feel as they feel. Only as we make that kind of identification ourselves can we get people to tread the Christian path.

But we have another powerful emotional aid to add to our soul-winning equipment: rapport. Its use is our next topic of discussion.

9

Play Yourself Down

Some scholars suggest that when the apostle Paul faced the learned men of Greece on Mars' hill, he was every inch the professor. His speech (Acts 17:22-31), some commentators would say, was almost arrogant in tone. He accused the Greek philosophers of being too religious and referred to their "ignorance." Predictably, he just got their backs up, and his mission in Athens was almost a complete failure.

But notice Paul's attitude at Corinth. "I, . . . when I came to you, came not with excellency of speech or of wisdom. . . . And I was with you in weakness, and in fear, and in much trembling" (1 Cor. 2:1-3). And in Corinth he was a tremendous success.

At Corinth, Paul most certainly played himself down. I had to learn to play myself down, too. At first, my insecurity made my ego intrude too much. I tended to display my knowledge, argue too much—the porcupine approach.

As time went on, soul-winning ceased to be an ego encounter. I only wanted to win people for Jesus' sake. The following instance shows the technique I ultimately developed.

The wife of a college professor had visited the church, so I made a courtesy call at her house. She was not at home,

Play Yourself Down

but her husband was. He could not have been more unreceptive. His attitude was sarcastic, hostile. I could sense his insecurity.

"So you're the man with all the degrees. I guess you want to teach a thing or two to a lowly educator."

"Haven't you heard that jack-of-all-trades is master of none?" I asked. "That's me! My wife tells me I would be better off if I had less education and more common sense. You wouldn't believe it, but I can't even put a set of bookshelves together without their falling part."

He grinned. "I know what you mean," he said.

His hostility started to evaporate. All it took was a bit of self-abasing banter. It succeeded in gaining the rapport I needed.

Rapport is simply emotional receptivity, the feeling of mutual goodwill and trust that makes a person open to new suggestions.

But it is important to realize that rapport is usually something that has to be introduced. It is not there in the first place. And it is also important to realize that the natural reaction to any approach is to be against it.

The reason for the problem lies in the ego drive, which was discussed at length in chapter 5. There it was seen that it is a matter of great concern to all of us to find and maintain ego fulfillment. The trouble is that everybody else is involved in the same search. Thus life is a competitive struggle in which some win and some lose. The other person is always a potential threat to our own ego, and his approach to us represents a possible ego crisis. Consequently, our guard is up. We become mentally alerted to fight off the intruder, and any suggestions he may make.

The sensible thing would be for us to make a distinction between a person and his ideas. Logically, when a person gives us a new idea, we gain rather than lose. But the emotions do not react logically. They treat the acceptance of the idea as a victory over our ego by the other person. Consequently, we fight it.

The degree of rejection varies enormously. It varies from gullibility on the one hand to outright negativeness on the other. One person might well believe that the moon were made of green cheese, if we told him. Another would insist that black were white, just because we said otherwise. The reaction varies with the extent to which the suggestion is seen to represent an ego threat.

Whether it does or does not represent an ego threat depends a great deal on the state of the ego war for the person concerned. In the case of the professor mentioned above, it turned out that he had been expecting to be made head of the department but had been passed by in favor of somebody else. That disappointment was a serious ego defeat and caused him to be all the more alert to the ego threat that I represented. Chances are that if he had been made department head, he would have been much more receptive to me.

The soul-winner cannot do much about the degree of ego sensitivity of the person he wants to approach about Christ. It will already have been determined by the person's state of fulfillment generally and by the prevailing circumstances. But the soul-winner can do a great deal to prevent the problem from becoming magnified. If he appears to be superior, arrogant, a know-it-all, there will be an immediate wall of resistance.

It is not enough for the soul-winner to be humble. He also must appear to be that way.

I know a young seminary student who was most anxious to win people but was rebuffed at every turn. Yet he was a nice enough person, humble and unassuming. The trouble was that his nervousness and anxiousness to succeed made him too abrupt, too intense. His approach was that of a personality commando raid, which quickly set up hostile defenses.

He was advised to relax, not to look upon a soul-winning encounter as putting his own ego on the line, but as laying a foundation on which the Holy Spirit could do the work. From then on his approach became casual and low key. As a result the encounter was no longer an ego threat. For the first time he started to win people.

Since, in our case, religion is the subject about which we approach people, we are especially vulnerable to poor rapport. Something about religion suggests that the Christian is somehow better than others. But that certainly is not a biblical idea, for salvation is an undeserved gift. Even Paul considered himself to be the chief of sinners. But that is not the way people think.

So when the soul-winner approaches a person, the immediate reaction is: "He thinks he's better than I am."

One man I particularly wanted to help was facing an embezzlement charge, and it had hit the newspapers. His reaction was predictably unfriendly.

"I guess you've come to save the jailbird."

"No, I couldn't even save myself. I needed God more than anybody. I still do. None of us is much better or worse than anyone else. It's just the problems that differ. No, I just wanted to see if there was anything I could do to help."

"I appreciate that," he sighed. "Sorry I sounded off. I guess I'm pretty up-tight."

That broke the ice right at the beginning. Often it takes longer. The man really needed help and support. As it turned out, the Lord gave him a great deliverance.

Another common ego barrier occurs when the person being approached gets the impression that the soul-winner is flaunting superior knowledge. It is an easy impression to give, because we have to be people of strong convictions to have any effectiveness at all. We are not expressing opinions or expounding theories, but presenting the Word of God. However, there is a difference between a dogmatic truth and a truth dogmatically put.

I found myself in a trap on this point once at the University of New Mexico in Albuquerque. Apparently I had waxed somewhat too eloquent on the superiority of Christianity to the religions of the East.

I was quickly confronted by a very irate student from India.

"You Americans take the cake for being arrogant," he said. "Why do you despise other religions? How come you think your country has a monopoly on truth?"

I felt very bad. I had not known he was there. It was a lesson in never making negative comparisons.

"Oh, I'm so sorry," I said. "I really didn't mean it that way. Christianity isn't from America; it came from Asia. I myself certainly do not have any claim on special knowledge. It's just that the Lord has been so good to me in allowing me to experience this faith. All I want is to share it with others.

"I tell you what. Come and drink a cup of coffee with me. I am interested in your religion and what you have experienced."

He was more than ready, his annoyance now quite gone. I did not have a chance to follow through on the encounter, as I was only visiting that city, but at least I had broken down his resistance.

Actually, something more than just ego reaction to an apparent know-it-all was involved. I had also violated his sense of loyalty. You certainly cannot get rapport that way. To avoid a loyalty problem, deal with truth for its own sake, and deal with error as error, without putting tags on

Play Yourself Down

it. Wherever we identify a point of view as being Roman Catholic, Protestant, Mormon, or Hindu, we are sticking our necks out. For one thing, we could be misrepresenting the group concerned. But even if what we say is correct, if our contact belongs to the group we are criticizing he will automatically take up arms in its defense. We have lost him.

As far as the talk that angered that Hindu student, I need not have mentioned Hinduism or the other religions at all. It would have been far better to have said that we Christians had tried to share our faith and the good life it brings with the people of the East.

Very often ego sensitivity generates an argument between the soul-winner and his contact. When that happens, rapport quickly evaporates.

I once got into such an argument with an atheist-Communist, while a Christian friend just listened. The atheist came out with some pretty destructive statements, so I just lit into him. Around and around we went, getting hotter under the collar all the time. Before long I had so angered him that I could not have sold him a loaf of bread if he had been starving.

It was the Christian friend who broke it up.

"I'm no good at philosophy, so I can't debate with you," he said. "But I would like to tell you what Christ has done for me."

The atheist listened without saying a word. I could see the message was getting through. By confessing his limitations at the start, my friend had effectively broken down the ego wall.

One important way of guaranteeing rapport is to make the other person's ego feel secure. And to make his ego feel secure we have to recognize that his point of view is important. If we need to change his point of view, we have to let him save face.

Once when I tried to witness to a student who turned out to be a Communist, I got a quick and smug rejoinder: "Religion is the opium of the people."

I felt my hackles rise. For one thing, I was tempted to tell him that the quotation should use the word *opiate,* not "opium." I did not. Not only would that have been quibbling, but also his ego would have resented being corrected.

I also wanted to tell him how much good Christianity had done for the world. I did not. That would have flatly contradicted him and been a signal for ego war.

Instead I said, "Yes, I'm afraid that that has often been the case. You're so very right. Isn't it a sad commentary on the human race that we prostitute God's good gifts?

"I'm sure you want to be constructive," I went on. "How do you think we Christians could use the wonderful truths Jesus taught for the good of humanity?"

"Gosh, I really don't know enough about Christianity."

He had now given me an excellent opening to go ahead with my message. His back was not up. He was eager to listen.

So much depends on the soul-winner's self-control at the first words of encounter. To protect his ego, the contact may be negative, argumentative, or abusive. We must never respond in kind. Somehow we have to realize that the attack is not personal and try to pour oil on the troubled waters. We have to make him feel good at the start so that he feels no need to put up his guard.

The example about the college professor showed how outright hostility was neutralized by a little lighthearted banter. Even where there is no hostility, a touch of humor is always useful in producing good rapport.

Public speakers employ humor all the time. An uninterested audience can quickly be turned into a receptive one by a suitably placed joke, especially if the joke is on the speaker himself. Laughter is most effective in neutralizing ego resistance.

One man told me he was afraid of using humor because he felt that the levity would detract from the seriousness and dignity of his message. Not so. Of course, being too jocular or acting like a clown would certainly do just that. The lighthearted touch done in good taste is what is needed.

Instead of lessening the impact of the message, this kind of humor adds to the force. It has been said that the quickest way to make an audience cry is to get them to laugh just before. Laughter brings the tragic or the serious into sharper relief.

So whether it is a first contact or someone we have known for ages, the approach should be casual, almost offhanded. For a few minutes it is best to let the conversation drift at will, peppering it with wit and fun. Not for long, however, or the person will get restless. Once the ice is broken, we can get to the point of the visit, depending on the circumstances. It is not hard to do.

"Oh, it's so nice to talk with you. What I really came about was to share with you something that has become very important to me—"

Above all, it pays to smile at the start and keep up a pleasant, easygoing manner.

Getting easy rapport takes only a little thought and care, but it largely determines whether the message gets through. Even if the message gets through, though, its acceptance does not follow of necessity. But the person will really listen, with his heart as well as with his mind.

Whether he will ultimately take that final step into the arms of Christ may depend on many factors. One of them could easily be his sense of guilt. Let us take a look at the guilt factor.

10

Zero in on the Feeling of Guilt

Nowhere in the Bible is soul-winning skill so evident as in the story of the woman at the well. The woman had been living an atrocious life and Jesus knew it. But instead of accusing her directly, He put it obliquely: "Go, call thy husband." That simple request zeroed in on the guilt in her soul. Shamefacedly she said, "I have no husband." Jesus said quietly, "Thou hast well said . . . for thou hast had five husbands; and he whom thou now hast is not thy husband" (John 4:16-18).

Later, when she told the men of her city about Jesus, she put it: "A man, which told me all things that ever I did" (John 4:29). He had spoken to her guilt.

Until we find Christ, guilt is a corroding misery to most of us. Take the case of Gerald.

He was about forty years old when I met him. A sensitive man, he had violated his conscience atrociously for years. Now it all had caught up with him. His wife had divorced him, and he was in trouble with the law. Self-revulsion and guilt were eating his insides out.

I let him talk out his misery and then, when he became calm, I repeated the verse: "The blood of Jesus Christ his Son cleanseth us from all sin" (1 John 1:7). I do not think I have ever seen such a feeling of release sweep over a man as when the significance of God's forgiveness hit him through those words. Almost instantaneously the burden had lifted, and with it the agony of guilt. Gerald was a transformed man.

I could not begin to count the number of times that I have used that particular verse. It carries tremendous impact because it is the balm of Gilead to the guilty soul. The offer of cleansing and forgiveness acts like a magnet to people plagued by self-disgust from their own wrongdoing.

Apparently we are made in such a way that sin is always followed by guilt. Not everybody feels guilt, but it is always there corroding the soul. Even the most sophisticated do not escape.

When Arlis came to see me, I was immediately impressed by her self-assurance and competence. In her forties, she was a successful college lecturer in journalism. She had been referred to me because of a deteriorating nervous condition.

Arlis had been brought up in a fundamentalist background, and she now despised it. She actually boasted of her new maturity: drinking and promiscuity.

But as the therapy proceeded, her unconscious mind told a different story. In her real self she was as square as they come, so her mind was revolting against behavior that was totally out of character. The guilt was there, but it was unconscious.

Finally she came to terms with herself and admitted that she really knew she was doing wrong. Now a much humbler (and nicer) person, she accepted the Lord's forgiveness. Her nerve symptoms quickly disappeared.

This hidden kind of guilt may at times be at the bottom of intellectual difficulties. When I was a student, one fellow showed interest in Christianity, yet he would always bring up some obstacle to faith. First it was creation, then

Noah's ark, then the plagues in Egypt, and so on. As soon as we would succeed in solving one problem, he would come up with another.

It was well known that he was living a pretty wild sex life at the time. At last, I figured that it might be the real trouble. I challenged him on the matter.

He quibbled a bit at first, rather lamely trying to justify his actions. I did not attempt to argue with him, so after a little while there was silence.

Then he said, "Aw, it's no use. I might as well admit it. I'm disgusted with myself, really."

He put the matter right and found inner peace. A little later he said, "Funny thing, those intellectual difficulties don't seem to have any force anymore."

The guilt of his sin had been blinding the eyes of his mind.

It has been said that a lot of so-called atheism is the wishful thinking of inner guilt. The unconscious mind of the sinner feels guilty; so, to avoid punishment, it abolishes God in the mind.

Of course, hidden guilt is not always the cause of intellectual problems. And it would be inexcusable to accuse a seeker who has problems with faith of some secret sin that is blinding his eyes. But the knowledge that hidden guilt can be an obstacle to faith is worth keeping in mind.

A curious feature of guilt is that it is associated in the mind with punishment—so much so that a person may not be able to accept forgiveness until he feels that punishment has been meted out.

I know that the need to see punishment administered was particularly true in my own case. As a teenager I did not really have that much to be guilty about; yet I was very much aware of my natural sinful state. I can remember that

Zero in on the Feeling of Guilt

I even tried to bargain with God: if He would cancel my sin, I would spend my life as a missionary.

What gave me peace was the doctrine of the substitutionary death of Jesus. The punishment had already been inflicted. Jesus had died instead of me, wiping out my own penalty.

To me, the substitutionary death of Jesus is the essence of the Good News anyway; so I often use it as a main selling point. It presents a kind of back door to the person's heart in terms of the need to deal with guilt. It is hard to tackle guilt directly unless the contact is consciously suffering from it. But telling the significance of the cross acts on latent guilt.

Here is what happened with a Texas redneck I once encountered. (He called himself that.) Successful, self-sufficient, tough, he was no more conscious of guilt than one of his steers was, at least, on the surface.

"Tell me, what is in this religion business for me?" he asked.

"Only you can answer that," I said. "But I can tell you what it has done for me. I was wide open to the wrath of God because of my sin. Jesus went ahead and suffered the penalty for me. You have no idea how nice it is to know that there can be no double jeopardy at the Judgment Day. I'll be as clean as a hound's tooth."

He did not say anything for a moment, and then he looked out toward the horizon as if he were visualizing that other world. Then he said, "Come to think of it, I am a mite uneasy about the judgment myself. Talk on, preacher."

The idea of washing or cleansing is closely allied to feelings of guilt. Compulsive hand-washing goes back far beyond *Macbeth* to Pontius Pilate. Our hands execute our deeds, so we feel that they are stained when we do evil. This feeling creates the compulsion to wash our hands even though we know that no physical action can wash away our evil. For the soul-winner, washing is a good symbol to use.

I once had a patient who was in bad mental shape because of guilt. While in military service, he had engaged in a homosexual act.

"I feel so dirty," he said.

I told him the Lord would forgive him, but he kept repeating, "But I feel so dirty."

"Yes, but the blood of Christ will wash you whiter than snow," I said. I stressed the word "wash," then repeated "whiter than snow."

I could see immediately that I had hit the spot. His face glowed.

"Oh, I would like that," he said. "I would like that so very much."

The substitution of "wash" for "forgive" made all the difference.

Incidentally, the use of the symbolism of washing is most effective in dealing with those who suffer from guilt due to sexual sins, which are looked upon as being particularly dirty.

Of course the great emphasis of the Bible is on the need for salvation from sin in general (that is, from sin as a state of the whole being) rather than from particular incidents of sin. Yet psychologically it is very difficult to bring conviction about sin in general. It is necessary to focus on particular sins that are concrete enough to bring about a feeling of guilt and then transfer the feeling to the whole sorry spiritual state.

Sometimes the sin can be very trivial. During the early part of World War II, I was present at a meeting where we

Zero in on the Feeling of Guilt

were telling our experiences as young Christians. The leader shared that before he became a Christian he used to use his employer's stamps to mail his personal letters, but now he knew that that was stealing.

A little later a girl burst into tears. "I've been stealing stamps, too," she sobbed, "and I want the Lord's forgiveness."

We quickly told her that the Lord could not do that unless she also sought forgiveness for her total sinful state. He needed her whole life, not just her attitude toward postage stamps. She was quite willing. Apparently it was no problem for her to take the extra step.

Our own confessions can be most effective in producing guilt in the person to whom we are speaking. For one thing, they do a great deal to lessen the ego resistance previously described in this book; and for another, they highlight his problem without giving offense.

One rather arrogant woman said to me, "You talk about salvation as if you had been saved from the guilt of murder or something. Come now, in your sheltered life, what could you have done to deserve all this fuss?"

Actually, my life had been far from sheltered, but there was no point in arguing about that.

"Well," I said, "Jesus taught that anger was murder, and I sure had my share of that. At the least provocation I would explode like a firecracker and create havoc all around me. I tried to master it, but I couldn't. Then the Lord stepped in. He did what I couldn't do."

She bit her lip. "You had no way of knowing it, but that is my soft underbelly too," she said. "I just can't control my temper. I never have been able to. I could cut my tongue out for the things I say when I get mad. You know, I think you may have something to say to me."

However, we have to be careful about this witness type of confession. If it goes beyond the restrictions of delicacy, it can cause revulsion.

One student used to witness that the Lord had saved her after being sexually promiscuous. Now if she were talking to another person with the same problem, it could help. But she used it as an opener with all her contacts, and it put them off.

When another person has been involved with the witness in the sin being confessed, and that person can be identified, courtesy demands that one should never mention it. One man had a wonderful conversion and was most anxious to witness. He readily confessed he had been committing adultery. The trouble was that he had been especially friendly with a particular girl, so everybody knew whom the adultery had been with. The man's witness was a shocking breach of sensitivity.

Although, as we have seen earlier, it is a mistake to witness about guilt we feel from trivialities, we should never belittle such guilt in others. We may well feel that a person is needlessly hung up on a trifle; yet that trifle may be indicative of something more serious, about which the person may have a wrong attitude or a right one.

One of the things that used to be stressed as undesirable in the church in which I was brought up was worldliness of dress. The fad for young fellows at that time was enormously wide trouser legs. One boy had a pair given to him but could find no peace of mind until he had had them altered to a more orthodox style.

Now I am sure that God was not interested in the width of trouser legs, but He was interested in that boy's attitude. The trousers had become a matter of conscience, which should always be obeyed. If that boy had done otherwise, he would have been choosing what he felt to be wrong. The guilt would not have been in the tailoring but in the rebellious attitude.

I once heard a Salvation Army captain make the astounding statement that she had not been able to become a Christian until she had been willing to go to hell. For her it had been the hang-up in her surrender to Christ. Those who dealt with her missed the point by insisting that there was no way in which God would want her to go to hell. The crisis was her unwillingness to do *anything* that God might ask; the unrealistic possibility was merely the focal point.

So when we are trying to win a person who has some trivial or improbable problem, we should not minimize it. It is a symptom of his struggle to commit himself to Christ; therefore he does have to surrender at that test point. I usually refer him to the story of Abraham and the sacrifice of Isaac, where God did not require the son's death but did absolutely insist on the father's willingness to sacrifice his son.

As we have seen, the problem of guilt usually focuses on concrete cases, and they become our lead into the basic problem of the person's sinful and, therefore, needy state. But it is important to stress that it is not only true that all our sins are forgiven, but that the principle of sin has been dealt with.

George had missed that distinction. He made his decision for Christ at an evangelistic meeting on Saturday night. But at the Christian Endeavor meeting the following morning, he was in near panic.

"I've lost it," he said. "I've sinned again. I got mad with my brother."

We explained to him that the blood of Christ had dealt with his sin *in principle,* covering all sins, whether past, present, or future.

"It's like your relationship with your father," someone said. "Once you are his son, your chance misdeeds do not cancel your sonship, they merely mar the fellowship for the time being."

One final point on this matter of guilt. Sometimes we have to draw a distinction between objective guilt and subjective guilt. Objective guilt is really being guilty. Subjective guilt is merely feeling guilty. I have seen a great number of new converts who still feel guilty, even though their objective guilt has been removed.

Adele was like that. She had had a pretty messed-up life and a lot to be guilty about. When she accepted Christ, everything seemed fine, but she came back very discouraged.

"It doesn't work," she complained. "I still feel as guilty as ever."

"What you feel like has nothing to do with it. The Word of God says that all your sins are washed away; so they are no longer there. You are feeling guilt about something that does not exist. You have accepted Christ; so now just accept His forgiveness."

It took a while, because feeling guilty had become a habit, but finally peace came.

Incidentally, it is worthwhile remarking that my experience as a clinical psychologist has shown me that guilt is one of the most agonizing of all mental illnesses. Therefore, when we use the gospel to eradicate it, we are making a tremendous contribution to human happiness.

Anyway, guilt is a negative thing. For a change, let us now study something on the positive side: the power of suggestion.

11

Use the Power of Suggestion, but Use It Responsibly

One of the most intriguing factors of Paul's genius is the way he could transform a defense of his own life and freedom into a soul-winning attempt. His trial before Agrippa is a graphic example. After paying a compliment to the king, he appealed to the prophets as his authority, and then, in a subtle touch, he managed to put across the suggestion that belief in the prophets implied belief in Jesus. It nearly worked, for Agrippa said: "Almost thou persuadest me to be a Christian" (Acts 26:28).

Paul's was a good use of the power of suggestion: the reinforcement of truth. But the power of suggestion can be bad.

A pastor had just returned from visiting the last of six people who had made decisions at an evangelistic meeting the night before. I had been there myself and had not liked it at all. Emotion had been heated up until the whole atmosphere was hypnotic. The appeal had been prolonged and pressured. Yet there had been considerable response.

"Not one of those cards was any good," he said. "Those converts were phony, not even interested the day after. I'm convinced the power of suggestion has no place in evangelism."

His reaction is only too typical, and for good reason. Evangelism has always been a fertile field for racketeers. Unscrupulous people are making millions out of it right now. The press calls them *spellbinders,* an apt term. They use the power of suggestion to throw a spell over the mind, forcing the person to do things that deep down he does not agree with at all.

Yet the pastor's reaction is still quite unwarranted. It is throwing out the baby with the bath water.

Since the power of suggestion was placed in our human makeup by the Creator, it has to be good in itself. But like almost all of God's great gifts, it can be prostituted to evil use. On the other hand, it can be a power for good. In particular, it can be a most important tool in the soul-winning equipment.

The danger of misuse is not so great in person-to-person evangelism as it is with meetings, because there is no crowd effect to amplify it. In any case, if the soul-winning venture is an earnest attempt to help people, and not an ego trip, there will be little problem.

I have often heard it advocated that cold-blooded reasoning is the only justifiable method. At first sight, that method does seem to carry a great deal of weight. The person approached is making a decision only on the merits of the case.

But it is not that simple. I remember one person who was trying to persuade me to this point of view who was very far from limiting himself to cold logic. He was emotional, forceful, and dogmatic. In fact, he was quite obviously using the power of suggestion to deny its use.

Actually, the only way to be completely cold-blooded in promoting a point of view is to have no interest in it at all. That attitude says, "Take it or leave it. It's no skin off my nose."

The Christian soul-winner certainly cannot be like that. He is very much aware of just how high the stakes are. The eternal destiny of a human being depends on the success of his efforts. The soul-winner should not *feel* casual about the matter; although, as we have seen, the *approach* should be studiedly casual. The approach is a different matter.

One of the most successful personal evangelists I have known was a young Irishman. He had an easygoing, charming, humorous approach, but he had a deep earnestness and sincerity in his faith. His power of suggestion, I would say, lay in the sense of conviction behind his words. Yet you never felt as if he were being dogmatic or fanatical.

Obviously, we always have to convince the person that our message is true. Truth itself, by its nature, is a matter of hard facts and rigorous logic, and emotion has no part in it. Yet even if something is true in fact, we are not always convinced it is true; that is, we do not always have psychological certainty. Also, unless we are convinced of a truth, it is not going to do us any good. The power of suggestion has a lot to do with changing logical certainty into psychological certainty, that is, changing actual truth into accepted truth.

I once met a man who claimed to have discovered a system that linked gravity with the earth's magnetic field. Try as I might, I could not flaw it, at least not on the first encounter. Yet I remained quite unconvinced. The trouble was the man himself. He was negative, argumentative, and arrogant. There was no suggestion of reliability about him, and therefore there was a strong suggestion that his theory was not reliable either.

In my early days in soul-winning, someone told me, "I don't know, but you don't ring true."

I think that a good deal of the problem was that I was

far too rapid and fluent a speaker. My words came out like a torrent and overwhelmed people. I sounded like a door-to-door salesman.

I learned to be more deliberate in my speech, leaving plenty of spaces for my contact to have his say or ask questions. I avoided giving any impression of insecurity, trying instead to generate an atmosphere of calm confidence.

Contrary to popular thinking, the gift of gab is no real advantage. An earnest person, halting and stumbling in speech, is often far more effective. It is obvious that his witness is costing him something, thus making a powerful suggestion that the gopsel is worth a great deal.

For our message to be convincing, it must be authoritative. We can achieve authority in two ways: by use of the Bible, and by the evidence of experience.

I used to know a tailor who told me that he made suits for a living, but that his real vocation was winning people for Christ. He was as good as his word and actually would go out searching for people to witness to. He had first thought out all the questions that he thought might be asked; then he found Bible verses that could answer them. He memorized the verses and then used them as the situations required.

Once he got a person interested, he would take him home and teach him from the open Bible. It was no wonder that his converts were so well informed and so definite about their faith.

Yet I also knew another young fellow who, instead of using the Scripture, merely parroted it. Somehow it sounded artificial.

The difference was that the tailor wove his verses naturally into his approach, taking care to paraphrase where the King James terms might not be understood. He still had his own way of putting things, but the Bible gave it substance and backing.

The second factor that tends to suggest authoritativeness to that which is already true in its own right is the voice of experience. It always carries tremendous weight when we can say, "I know it's true because it has happened to me."

Personal experience is especially applicable when we are dealing with a person who feels as if he is facing an impossible struggle in his own life. To him, everything we say sounds so theoretical.

"I understand how you feel," I said to a young alcoholic, "and I assure you that Christ can break your chains."

"No you don't!" he hotly retorted. "You've never been an alcoholic, so how can you say you understand?"

I had to admit he had a point, so I brought back an alcoholic whom the Lord had wonderfully delivered.

"I'm an alcoholic," he said. "But since I've been a Christian, I haven't touched a drink in twelve years."

The young fellow nodded his head. It was easy to see that he was convinced.

A few years after World War II, I was a leader in a religious-emphasis week at Linfield College. The barrage from disillusioned veterans was particularly tough.

One bearded veteran sounded like a prosecuting attorney. "You admit that the philosophical proofs for the existence of God are not conclusive?"

"Yes."

"You admit you can't demonstrate the existence of God by scientific means?"

"True."

"Then how can you, as an educated man, believe in God?"

"Because I am experiencing Him. I am as sure of His

existence as I am of yours. But don't believe it because I say so; find your own proof by your own confrontation with Him."

"I may do just that," he said. "There's something convincing about what you say that rings a bell."

It should be added that absolute honesty is essential. We should be honest for no other reason than that it is right, but there is something more. If we witness to more than we have experienced, it sounds hollow and kills the suggestion of truth.

Shortly after my conversion, while I was still battling with the problem of bad temper, I testified in my youthful enthusiasm that God had given me the victory over my temper. Actually, I fully believed He would; but, although things had improved, it had not happened yet.

Later, one of our leaders said to me, "Jim, I had the feeling you were jumping the gun when you testified of victory over bad temper."

"I guess you've been talking with my parents," I said.

"No. I wouldn't do that. It's just that you sounded lame."

That experience taught me a lesson I shall never forget.

On the other hand, I do not mean that we have to wait for perfection in order to be able to witness. I only mean that we should never claim more than we have experienced at the time.

I once heard a converted drunk say, "The Lord has given me a wonderful victory over drink, but I'm afraid I'm still battling over cussing. Somehow it catches me unawares."

That man was very convincing indeed. Honesty always carries a strong suggestion of the truth that is being proposed.

Another factor that psychologists have found to be highly suggestible is, strange to say, repetition. If we repeat a

Use the Power of Suggestion, but Use It Responsibly

statement frequently, the chances of its being accepted are greatly increased.

Repetition is very noticeable in the teachings of Jesus. He would introduce a truth in the form of a short statement, go on to a general discussion, and then, after a few words, repeat the original statement word for word or almost word for word. It is most effective. For example: "He that hath ears to hear, let him hear" (Mark 4:9, 23); "I am the good shepherd" (John 10:11, 14); "I am the true vine" (John 15:1, 5); "This is my commandment, That ye love one another" (John 15:12, 17).

I have found that repetition is especially valuable when trying to persuade a guilt-laden person to accept forgiveness. As indicated in chapter 10, I make a lot of use of the verse, "The blood of Jesus Christ his Son cleanseth us from all sin" (1 John 1:7). When I find that acceptance is not going to be easy, I keep repeating that verse at intervals during the conversation, enunciating every word clearly and distinctly so that the verse stands out from everything else I say.

The problem of evil is another great difficulty that repetition helps me deal with. For example, I knew a young woman whose mother had developed cancer. She was devastated, angry, and bitter. "Why did God do this to my mother?"

It was hard to get through to her that God was not some malicious demon implanting cancers on unsuspecting people, that He was more anxious to see cancer eradicated than we were. I started my explanation by stating, "God does not cause evil; He's not like that." Between every point, and after every interjection on her part, I would repeat those words slowly and deliberately.

At last she sighed. "I guess that in my heart I must have

known God had to be good, not evil. I can see that clearly now. Maybe He'll help the doctors save Mom."

We have seen that there is powerful suggestive force in the soul-winner's confidence in his message. The same is true for his confidence that his effort to win somebody will be successful. Our case is greatly helped when the person approached can see that we except him to respond positively.

The reverse is particularly true. We are all aware of the negative effect of such statements as "You wouldn't want to buy a vacuum cleaner, would you?"

I must confess that my first approach to professional people was almost that bad. I was apologetic, expecting to be rebuffed, and fearful of the counterthrust of their high intelligence. I did not really expect to be successful, and, of course, I was not.

My approach was usually to anticipate what I believed would be the inevitable intellectual difficulties. A medical student's remark changed my approach. He interrupted me by saying, "The miracles of the Bible are not what's bothering me. My problem is that I am riddled with anxiety for fear I won't make it as a doctor."

My lack of confidence in reaching him about the needs of his soul had put me completely off the wavelength of his needs.

I realized then the truth of what has been well put by Billy Graham: "The needs of an Oxford don are no different from those of a Pennsylvania coal miner."

After that, when I approached a professional man I would tell myself: "He's just an ordinary sinner like me, in need of the gospel of Jesus." Since then there has been no apologetical attitude.

"Doctor, I want to share with you that Christ has given me the solution to the problems of living and provided me

Use the Power of Suggestion, but Use It Responsibly 103

with something worth living for. He can do the same for you, and I feel sure that you will feel this way if you can give me a few minutes of your time."

Obviously, the approach to the coal miner would not need to be any different.

I do not mean that we are going to win every time we try. Neither should we expect to. But we should approach every person feeling confident that we have a message that he can readily accept. We have to feel that he is crazy not to, and then the chances are that he will feel the same way.

Psychologists have also found that the effectiveness of the power of suggestion also depends on the potential convert's being part of a group who already believe. The pitch of the Communists apparently becomes most persuasive at party meetings, even though it is only a repetition of what has been said in private. Salesmen are most easily recruited at sales meetings.

Thus if we can succeed in taking the person we want to win to mingle with a group of convinced Christians, our message will carry much greater impact because the suggestion is greater.

Taking him to church is one way of attempting to get him in with a group of Christians, but a church situation does not have as great an influence as, say, a seminar. In the seminar there is the cumulative effect of the faith of each individual if it is expressed or indicated individually. In a church service there is not that multiple individual expression.

Jim was an agnostic; yet he seemed to be trying hard to believe. No matter how I tried, I could not get him to take the step of faith.

"What you say is logical enough," he would say. "I can't fault it, but somehow I'm not quite convinced."

I took him to a Christian group. For a couple of hours

people from various walks of life testified of their faith. Afterward he said, "OK, you win. That was overwhelming."

Apparently it is not just the cumulative force of the words of a group that carries the power of suggestion; the crowd effect is also important. In some mysterious way, a group that is united toward a common goal develops an impact far above the sum of what each person would have individually. We can use the total crowd effect with wonderful results.

I started this chapter by indicating that the power of suggestion is open to terrible abuses by the unscrupulous. It can also be misused by the conscientious soul-winner. He will not want to use it as a weapon to bludgeon the mind; but even if he does act responsibly, the results can be shallow.

What is always needed is the undergirding of such decisions by careful nurturing. The convert has not come to his decision by a chain of reasoning; so we shall need to provide him with a reason for his faith. Thus his commitment will be solidly based and will reach to the depths of his personality.

We can conclude then that, rightly used, the power of suggestion is a most valuable soul-winning aid to add to the helps previously described. Of course, in practice, the techniques used in any particular case may well be a combination of the psychological devices we are studying.

The soul-winner's goal is to change attitudes, and attitudes are generally so complex that such a multiple attack is necessary. Once again psychology can come to our aid, since a vast amount of research has been carried out on the problem of attitude change. The following chapter will show how relevant to the soul-winner some of that research is.

12

Reverse That Negative Attitude

Nobody could have had a more seething hatred for Christianity than the apostle Paul before his conversion. It would be impossible to imagine a less likely prospect for Christian conversion. Yet in that encounter on the Damascus Road (Acts 9:3-22), hate was changed to fervent love, and opposition to dedicated service.

Negative attitudes are easier to reverse than we might think.

I mentioned earlier that I was dead wrong in my early days as a soul-winner in assuming that intellectuals or professional people would be especially difficult to win. I was also wrong in another presupposition: that hostile people should be avoided. As it has turned out, the hostile person has often proved to be easier to persuade than the indifferent person. Also, he makes the better Christian once he is converted.

The problem is how to change or reverse an emotionally charged attitude. Fortunately, scholars have accumulated a great deal of psychological data about such changes. Attitude change is so vitally important to the politician and the advertiser that millions of dollars have been spent on research about it. Having become acquainted with this work almost from the start, I have used it extensively and profitably. I want to share some examples of how the soul-winner can use this knowledge.

Zen came from one of the Central European countries. Bulgaria, I think. He was vigorously socialistic, but he was not a Communist; he held typical Marxist antireligion views. His goal in life was to see the world become a federation of socialist republics on the Scandinavian model.

"I want a whole new system, and the church is in the way," he said. "It has got to go."

"You sound like Jesus," I said. "He wanted a new order, too, and felt that organized religion in His day was an obstacle."

"Jesus, a socialist?"

"Wrong. Jesus was no 'ist' of any kind. His point was that no system will work without changing people first. He tries to make them to be like Himself: loving, kind, and interested in the needs of others."

"Come on now; the church has not been like that. It has exploited people. Look at South America."

"You are so right. He has had to try to get through to His own followers. But you can't blame Him for their failures."

"But you said He changed people."

"He does when they let Him, but He won't burglarize their wills to do so, as in brainwashing. Anyway, you don't blame socialism for bad socialists, do you?"

"No. I guess not."

"I tell you what, Zen. You are a fair man. Go for yourself and find out what Jesus really did teach. Read through the gospel of Mark. You can do it in about an hour. Then we'll talk again."

"Fair enough."

He was as good as his word. We had many talks after that. His very intensity drove him to search out the matter

Reverse That Negative Attitude

thoroughly. He would not let the thing rest until he had a verdict. When it came, it was for Christ. The day after he made his decision, he applied to a Bible college.

In Zen's case, psychology would indicate that there were two things necessary to change his attitude: neutralize his hostility, and redirect the force of his emotion.

As is so often the case, Zen's antagonism was disarmed by agreeing with him and, in this case, by showing that Jesus felt the same way about exploitation by religious bodies. The wrong thing to have done here would have been to get sidetracked into countering his obvious unfairness (since the church certainly has not been totally bad in its social relationships). Such an attempt would only have increased his hostility.

Also, I think I succeeded in redirecting the force behind his antagonism. First I teased him into a vigorous search into the teachings of Jesus. When he saw what Jesus taught, he himself rechanneled his drive. So what I did was similar to what a sailor in a sailboat does when he uses adverse winds to his advantage.

I said earlier that we have to take a hard look at intellectual difficulties bceause they may merely be a cover for a hidden emotional problem. However, quite often real, honest intellectual problems do occur and have to be dealt with sympathetically. They are most formidable when there are several of the same kind.

Psychological research has shown that each of a string of objections not only has weight in its own right, but also tends to reinforce all the others. Suppose I have some evidence of a man's dishonesty. I may overlook his dishonesty, but not if I find more evidence. The case then becomes overwhelmingly convincing. The reason is that we think we see a common pattern.

A string of intellectual objections to faith has the same

sort of cumulative effect. To overcome it, we should not have to attend to each item in the string; rather, we should find a common factor that will neutralize the total impact. Let me illustrate.

Sam was over seventy. He prided himself on his intellectual honesty. He would have liked to be a Christian, but he said that he had a problem with the Old Testament miracles.

"If it were just one miracle," he said, "it wouldn't bother me so much, but there are so many of them: crossing the Red Sea, the walls of Jericho, Joshua's long day, the ax that floated for Elisha, and many more. It adds up to a total atmosphere of myth and legend. That's no place for an educated man."

"It boils down to whether you believe in God," I said.

"There's no problem there. Of course I believe in God. I always have. It's those miracles."

"But how can you believe in a supernatural God who can't do supernatural deeds?"

He was silent for the longest time. Then he nodded. "I see what you mean. I've been missing the point. Maybe I've been looking at miracles in isolation. *You* see them as God in action. I think you may have solved my problem."

There was no need then for Sam to go into the scientific feasibility of each individual miracle. He recognized the fact that with God all things had to be possible. He saw the common denominator.

Another type of resistance noted by psychologists is one that cannot be resolved by a single principle. It is present when the obstacles are unrelated. Then there is no escape from dealing with them one by one. But each problem that is successfully dealt with makes the next one that much easier.

For example, Cynthia was a graduate student in biology,

Reverse That Negative Attitude 109

and her resistance was pretty solid. Her reasons were explicit.

"I couldn't be a Christian," she said. "I believe in evolution, I wouldn't have the nerve to be baptized in public, and I don't want to be tied down."

In spite of her matter-of-fact rejection, I sensed that in her heart she really wanted to be persuaded; so I persevered with her. Each time I saw her I took up one of her problems, completely ignoring the others because I did not want them to gang up on her in her mind.

Of course, I did not go into the truth or falsehood of the theory of evolution. The last thing I wanted was an argument, especially in the area of her own expertise.

"Even if evolution were to be true," I said, "you still have to have a God to start things off in the first place. Even Darwin admitted that. It makes sense to me that the emphasis should be on God, not on His creation. Surely if we get in tune with Him personally, we are better able to understand all His works."

In the end she agreed that the whole evolution matter was pretty irrelevant to what really was at issue: her relationship to God.

As for the second obstacle, since she was from a Baptist background, it was baptism by immersion that she was balking at. I made the mistake of trying to make it easier for her by suggesting that she be baptized in private.

Her eyes blazed. "If I ever get baptized at all, it won't be in some secret closet but right in the open. I'm not that sort of woman."

I quickly got back on the right track by telling her that if she gave her heart to the Lord, He would give her the courage to do whatever He required. Finally she admitted that she had allowed baptism to become a "thing," as she put it, and she no longer raised it as an objection to her becoming a Christian.

That left the "tied down" issue.

"You are tied down now," I argued. "We all are tied down to something or the other. I don't know anything so confining as working for a higher degree. But you don't mind, because it's something you want. I'm tied down, too: to Christ, but I could not be more content. Your so-called freedom isn't making you that happy, is it?"

She resisted pretty hard, but somehow, as we talked, the problem seemed to evaporate.

Cynthia came around in time and committed her life to Christ. I thought she would need to talk over the three difficulties in the light of her decision, but she did not. She was too wrapped up in her new experience.

Another thing that research has made clear is that resistance to change is dependent on how vital to the person's needs the original position is. If it represents deep emotional satisfaction, we shall not be able to budge the person at all unless we can offer him an acceptable substitute.

Olive was being treated for a drinking problem. She was only in her thirties, a divorcée, and childless; and things had become pretty bad. Nothing seemed to help: AA, Antabuse, hospital "drying out," nothing. I was convinced that only a total spiritual rebirth could save her. In spite of help from converted alcoholics and my own positive assurance that Christ could transform her life, she would not give in.

She puzzled me because she seemed desperate enough to try anything. I began to suspect that there must be something more basic than alcohol at fault. We started therapy sessions.

Analysis showed that she was just plain scared: afraid to venture. So far, nearly everything she had attempted resulted in her being badly hurt. The drinking had hurt her, too, but not like the other things. It was a refuge. Nobody expected an alcoholic to achieve anything.

It was explained to her that her fear was nothing to be ashamed of. In fact, it was quite to be expected in the circumstances. What she needed to do was to come to terms with it; then it would not be emotionally crippling.

"I just can't face it," she said.

I told her the wonderful story of Mary Slessor, the great missionary to Equatorial Africa. As a girl in Scotland, Mary was paralyzed by fear. She was so timid that she would not venture out on firecracker night and would not walk through a field with a cow tied up in it. Yet God called her to face the terrors of that cannibal-ridden land. With the help of God, Mary mastered her fear. Later, she even put herself between warring tribes, compelling them to make peace.

"Do you really think God could do that for me?" Olive asked.

"Why don't we try Him?"

Olive made her confession, just trusting the Lord to handle her fear. At first she was very timid in venturing out, but soon she found that she could handle the problems of life. Eventually she became so self-assured that people could hardly believe she was the same person. She never drank again.

This requirement to defuse resistance by replacing the obsessive hang-up with something better is especially true for those with severe ego problems: the chronically insecure people. They have to be made to see that becoming a Christian can give them greater satisfying fulfillment than they have ever dreamed of.

Some studies on attitude change have revealed interesting differences. For instance, it has been found that blue-collar workers are more resistant than white-collar workers, men are more resistant than women, and emotionally calm people are more resistant than disturbed persons. My own experience bears out those findings.

A farm laborer and his wife came to an evangelistic crusade I conducted at a San Joaquin Valley town in the 1950s. They showed such interest that I visited them in their home, but I got nowhere.

After I talked the problem over with the pastor there, he immediately suggested sending the active church member who did the church's janitorial work out to talk with the couple. The man had no difficulty at all. The couple accepted the Lord and joined the church.

Now I do not think I have any particular problem achieving rapport with blue-collar people. It is just that they respond more easily to people who are in their own circumstances. In any case, as has been stated earlier, it is always easier when both parties are in similar walks of life. Probably the big reason blue-collar people are harder to change is because the one attempting to make them change is usually a white-collar worker.

The fact that women are easier to change than men is borne out by the greater number of women than men in so many of our churches. Women seem to sense spiritual realities more easily. Thus the best strategy for getting a foothold for Christ in a family may be to approach the women first. Such work is an excellent opportunity for our women's associations, by the way.

The finding that troubled people are especially suggestible to attitude change is most emphatically verified by experience. Great numbers of those I have led to Christ have been those whom I have met because they were in trouble. When we seek to help them in one area, that of their distress, it is not hard to lead them on to the greatest need of all.

If anyone really wants to win people for Christ and does not have the contacts, I suggest that he head for the hospitals and homes for the aged. He will find people who will not only welcome his coming, but who will be wide open to the gospel.

We have already seen a number of instances in which a group has been important in evangelism. The investigations on attitude change support the idea that a group can have an important part in evangelism. It has been shown that a person in a group tends to accept opinions that the group favors, especially if he has himself taken part in the group's discussions.

For instance, in an experimental seminar she attended, a housewife who normally used soap powder A changed to B, the product preferred by the others. She reported that a factor in her change was the leader's asking her how she thought the new product might be superior.

I have seen a similar thing happen in Christian work. It was at a Methodist retreat in the mountains of New Mexico. A wife had prevailed upon her reluctant husband, a doctor, to come with her. One of the seminars was on nervous troubles. I asked the doctor if he would mind saying a word or two as a physician on how he thought Christianity might help. He made a telling contribution.

Later I had a long talk with him. He said, "You know, I think I talked myself into it by what I said at that seminar." He accepted Christ.

I think churches should do far more of that sort of group evangelism, especially if it takes place away from the church premises, for example, in homes or at resorts. It is most effective.

One thing I have always wondered about is the usefulness of the public commitment, such as coming forward at the appeal in services. I have now found that psychological research favors it. The act tends to crystallize the change.

Thus, if a housewife says aloud to a group, "I am going to change to product B," she is much more likely to do so than if she does not make her intention public. Perhaps this crystallization of commitment is one of the great practical advantages of the church's requiring some kind of public confession.

Actually, I often use the prospect of an act of commitment as an opening to the soul-winning process. I might say something like this: "I think we are doing a pretty significant thing down at Coronado. We are making quite an impact on people's lives. I would like you to be part of what's happening there, to have you identify with us in membership. But before you do either of those things, we must first talk about your relationship to Christ."

Somehow the expressed goal of a definite act gives focus to the whole thing. It makes the matter tangible. Just to talk about conversion, without some physical expression of commitment in view, loses a lot of the impact.

I am well aware, of course, that persuading a person to turn from self and sin to Christ is far different from changing from one detergent to another or from one political party to the other; yet the psychological mechanisms involved are similar for any attitude change. The Lord of creation is remarkably consistent in His ways. The main thing is that we succeed in reversing the soul from its slide to eternal loss.

The preceding chapters summarize most of the applications of modern human-engineering techniques, as I am aware of them, to soul-winning. It now remains to tie the various strands together in an emphasis on the personal self-giving that is involved in winning people for Christ.

13

Love the Person You Want to Win

Earlier I mentioned that the story of the woman at the well exemplifies soul-winning at its best. Not only were the techniques Jesus used the best, but He evidenced His interest in her as a person. He loved her.

He seemed to be aware that she would feel honored if He asked for a drink from her: an outcast. He sensed the thirst in her soul. He dealt with her problem of guilt (as we saw in chap. 10). He sympathized with her confusion about where God should be worshiped. In announcing His Messiahship and in His emphasis on spirit, He treated her with as much dignity and importance as if she were a doctor of the Law.

When we love the person we want to win as Christ did, we can never be mechanical.

I hope that the insights of this book will never lead to the kind of attitude that allows us to perform in our minds the cold dissection of the psyche of the person we want to win for Christ. We shall be aware of his needs just as we are of our own, but we must remember that he is essentially a living person, not the mere sum of basic drives. Thus we shall approach him with the deepest respect, never trying to manipulate him.

Unfortunately, evangelism is not always that careful. I have heard evangelists talk of the number of souls they have saved in much the same way that a hunter brags of the ducks he has bagged.

In my own seeking days I talked with a number of evangelists after meetings. I wanted to explain my needs, to bare my soul, but they cut me off. They only seemed interested in getting a quick decision and hurrying on to the next person. Not one of them first asked my name.

We have to keep in mind that soul-winning is a penetration into another person's inner life. As such, it is an awesome responsibility. It should be done only with the deepest sense of personal delicacy and with the utmost care for his sensitive feelings.

This type of soul-winning involves a great deal of self-giving. It is never enough to give only our knowledge or experience. We have to give ourselves. We develop a personal bond of love and care with our contact in the hope that out of it will come a relationship with our Lord.

It is important to realize that our relationship with our contact is no temporary one—it is no mere device to use and then discard. If we are truly interested in him, we shall want to know him as a person and therefore shall expect the friendship to last.

What I have just said does not necessarily mean that every soul-winning contact will develop into one of those intimate relationships that all of us need, at least to some extent. Close relationships depend on specific characteristics that are peculiar to our needs and that not many people have.

Although our relationship with our contact may never be an intimate one, it can still be one of a hundred friendships that cause our hearts to glow at the thought of them. The actual encounters may not be frequent, but our friend knows and we know that we can depend on each other when necessary. Anything else is artificial and unsatisfying and can be an affront to one's personality.

That reminds me sadly of George. In his late teens, he was not as bright as most, and he found friends hard to come by. He was won by a dedicated, intense person in our group who went to all kinds of trouble to win George: he took him to games, invited him home, and cultivated a real friendship. Soon George would have done anything for him. But George's conversion ended the friendship. The soul-winner was off after other game.

"He doesn't seem to want me anymore," said George. "I thought he was my friend."

It was heartbreaking. Of course, that degree of friendship could not very well be kept up. The trouble was that it was artificial in the first place. That soul-winner did not really want George's company. The friendship was merely a come-on. It would have been much better if the relationship had been lower key in the first place. It should have been a sincere expression of mutual desires.

Suppose that we decide to take a man to dinner as a step toward winning him for Christ. That can either be a cheap salesman's trick or a lovely gesture. It is justified only if we have such an interest in him that we feel that we, too, can gain from the association, that we want to be with him and enjoy his friendship.

If we feel that way, we certainly shall not be able to drop him once he has become a Christian. In other words, we shall be loving him.

When we love a person and respect him, it will be impossible for us to mechanically apply psychological devices to make him do what we want. Our knowledge of those techniques will simply be the means we use to understand him so we can be a better friend. In the light of that concern, we can suggest to him how the Savior can meet his deepest needs.

So what we soul-winners are actually doing is building up lifelong friendships. If we are not prepared to be that involved, we are not ready to be soul-winners at all.

A price is to be paid for that kind of involvement. We must have a deep concern for the welfare of an increasing number of people, and sharing sorrows is not easy.

I suppose a great number of those won at Coronado have been through my efforts. They seem to be more than my church members; they are more like part of my family. Wherever I go for the rest of my life, what happens to each one will be a matter of deep concern to me. Whenever they have suffered, I have suffered with them.

This book is about personal evangelism. I think it is the only way an effective church can be built. As I see it, the principles of personal evangelism are as true for the pastor as they are for the layman.

I once was the minister of a large church. To my chagrin, I was largely an administrator. Most of my days were spent behind a desk, and most of my nights were spent in tedious committee meetings. There were budgets to raise, causes to promote, business to transact, but there was very little time for people.

As I have described in chapter 1, when we started Coronado Christian Church, I determined it would not be like that. I wanted to be with people, and that is the way it has been.

I think some of those first members were dubious; no church they had known had been run in such a way. Yet the church prospered There has always been sufficient money, and everything has gone smoothly. Apparently, most of the business that a minister and his officers are involved in, with such terrible consumption of time, energy, and money, may not be necessary after all. We can get on perfectly well without it.

So I have spent my time with individuals—in their homes, in their offices, in hospitals, or wherever I could find them. There has never been any high pressure, just the quiet development of friendships; but out of those friendships came discipleship with Christ.

I think that is how the ministry ought to be. I would like to see concerned laymen cut their ministers loose from the business trappings so that they, too, could have the satisfaction I have found.

I would dearly like to see Christianity get back to the individual in all aspects. By its very nature, there is no way in which it can be mass produced. Radio and TV might saturate the world with the gospel message, but that saturation would not, in itself, win people. Winning people can only come through person-to-person contact. First we experience the miracle of transformation by the indwelling Christ, and then we share it with others.

It is just as simple and as profound as that.